The Household
of faith

The Household
of faith
The changing pattern of the church's life

T. Ralph Morton

WILD GOOSE PUBLICATIONS

IONA COMMUNITY CLASSICS

To Jenny
to whom it owes so much
and I so much more

Copyright © 1951 & 2005 The Iona Community

First published 1951
Reprinted 1952
2nd edition 1958
3rd edition 2005, published by
Wild Goose Publications, Fourth Floor, Savoy House,
140 Sauchiehall Street, Glasgow G2 3DH, UK,
the publishing division of the Iona Community.
Scottish Charity No. SCO03794.
Limited Company Reg. No. SCO96243.

ISBN 1-905010-04-4
ISBN13 978-1-905010-04-2

All rights reserved. No part of this publication may be reproduced in any form or by any means, including photocopying, electronic publishing or any information storage or retrieval system, without written permission from the publisher.

A catalogue record for this book is available from the British Library.

Printed by Digisource, Livingston EH54 8SJ

CONTENTS

	Page
Foreword	4

PART I
THE CHURCH

1. WHAT IS TO BE THE PATTERN OF THE CHURCH'S LIFE ? — 7
2. THE NATURE OF THE CHURCH — 13

PART II
THE CHANGING PATTERN OF THE CHURCH'S LIFE

1. IN THE BEGINNING — 21
2. THE HOUSEHOLD OF FAITH — 26
3. THE MONASTERY — 33
4. CHRISTENDOM — 41
5. THE CHRISTIAN FAMILY — 51
6. THE CONGREGATION — 61

PART III
THE TASK TO-DAY

1. THE CHANGING PATTERN IN THE PAST — 79
2. THE SITUATION WE ARE IN — 84
3. THE OTHER THING NEEDFUL — 94
4. THE EMERGING PATTERN — 98
5. THE THREE ESSENTIALS — 105
6. ECONOMIC DISCIPLINE — 114
7. THE HEART OF THE MATTER — 121
   Appendix I — 126
   Appendix II — 129

FOREWORD

THE IONA COMMUNITY, since its inception in 1938, has been concerned with the necessity of finding some new form of economic discipline. As the Community's primary task was in terms of the Church's mission to men in industry, and as that task was so soon seen against the background of a world war, it will easily be realised that this question of Christian economic discipline came to assume an even greater importance as the years passed. For to men who are convinced that their lives are economically determined, it is no use saying that man does not live by bread alone, unless we ourselves are truly seeking first the Kingdom of God and His righteousness and are convinced by the experience of our own lives that 'all these things' are added unto us. It was seen both as a crucial problem for the Church to-day, and first of all, as a problem to be dealt with in our own fellowship. The Community would not claim to have found the way. All it can claim is to be more than ever convinced that the way must be found. It is only as we are somehow expressing our faith in terms of our ordinary economic living that the Faith will be made intelligible to other men, for thus alone shall we come to understand its fulness ourselves.

This small book expresses the concern of the Community and something of its thinking. Economic discipline has been so constant a subject of discussion at our meetings, and so many have contributed to that discussion, that it is hard to disentangle what is the thinking of the Community from the expression and opinions of the author. The Community cannot be held responsible for all that is said

FOREWORD

in it: for its mode of expression and for its opinions I alone can accept responsibility. It is an essay: a tentative effort to express the general concern of the Community; to provoke thought and to stimulate action. It, therefore, seemed better to put it in a personal and perhaps too provocative a manner than to put it in the form of a carefully balanced report that has passed through the seive of resolutions and amendments.

But though I accept full responsibility for the opinions expressed in it, I cannot but say that whatever it contains of value is due to the heated discussions and prolonged study of the Community and, even more, to the experience that has been ours through living and working together. In particular it was out of the work of a committee which met week by week throughout the winter of 1947-48 that the main thought of this book emerged. It was then that we began to see something of the changing pattern of the Church's life through the centuries and to realise that this problem of finding an economic expression of the Faith was no new problem. We found we were faced with a larger task than we had envisaged when we were appointed to study the question of the Church's economic discipline to-day.

To the members of that Committee I should like to express my indebtedness: to David Johnston, Uist Macdonald, John MacMillan and Cameron Wallace.

Then in the staff meetings of Community House, Glasgow, in the autumn of 1949 we came to see more clearly the form of economic experiment that was possible for us. There is, therefore, much of our corporate life and of our study in this book.

And, for myself, I cannot but realise that without the experience of life in a missionary community in Manchuria during the early years of the Japanese occupation, I would not have seen the meaning of the Church as I now see it, or been in The Iona Community at all. Anything this book has to say is due to the experience of Christian community abroad and at home, which I have known to be a real thing in the world to-day.

To four others I would like to express my personal debt: to George MacLeod, the Leader of the Community, who saw the issue and stated it clearly when others were only fumbling and who has kept the Community true both to this central concern and to a realistic facing of the issues involved: to Penry Jones, the Industrial Secretary of the Community, for his encouragement and patient advice: to John Morrison, the manager of the Publications Department of the Community, without whose enthusiasm and resource this book would never have been published: and, first and last, to my wife whose understanding of the issues involved has been the main inspiration of my work and whose help in its execution has been my constant support.

T. R. M.

EDINBURGH,
Easter, 1951.

I

THE CHURCH

1. WHAT IS TO BE THE PATTERN OF THE CHURCH'S LIFE?

WHAT is to be the pattern of the Church's life? Or, to put that question more personally, how should Christians be trying to live in the world to-day?

That is a vital question. It is also the primary question. There are other questions which we prefer to discuss, because they seem bigger. There have been plenty of statements of the task of the Church in the world to-day and, provided they are general enough and big enough, they raise no questions. The trouble is not that the Church does not know its task, whether that task be put in terms of transforming society or of winning men or of declaring the truth. The trouble is that Christians do not see how they can carry it out. There have been even more descriptions of the world situation: diagnoses, political, economic, psychological, of the world's ills. But these do not seem to have helped the Church to know how to act but rather to have made Christians more aware of excuses for their failure than of repentance: more interested in the diagnosis of their own ills than confident of the world's cure. There have, in more recent years, been many attempts at defining more immediate objectives and drawing up programmes of strategy. Of such, the most interesting and the most necessary have been plans on the Continent and in this country for winning the workers to the Church. But, unless the target is within range and the programme workable, such attempts at defining objectives may be only frustrating and even dangerous. For to become more and more clear about what we ought to be doing and more and more aware that we are unlikely to do it is very dangerous: it dissolves our conviction in the things that we are doing and leaves our theorizing entirely in the air.

All these statements of the Church's task, all these descriptions of the world situation, all these definitions of objectives assume that the Church is the instrument ordained of God to carry out His purpose in the world. They all, indeed, assume that some reformation of the Church is necessary. But such reforms of the Church are deduced and secondary. Basic to all these discussions is surely the question: How can the Church become the fit instrument for that purpose?

That is the subject of this essay. Do we assume that the Church as we know it is that instrument? Do we think that, without giving any thought to its ability, without first seeing that the Church is as fitted as possible, the Church can set about its task? Or do we feel that something quite revolutionary is needed to make the Church a fitter instrument for these tremendous purposes? Is not the one responsibility laid upon us to see that we are faithful stewards? Is not that, in a sense, the only question about which we have to worry? We must, indeed, seek to understand the ultimate task of the Church, but it is not given to us to know the times or the seasons. We must, if we are serious, be concerned with the Church's strategy, but we can never know the future and are foolish to build on our foretelling of it. But it is given to us, and to no one else, to chose what kind of servants we will be. The outcome of our work is not in our hands, but the 'talents' are. We alone decide whether we shall bury our talent in a napkin or use it profitably. The Spirit of God is the life of the Church. His love and mercy must be mediated to men through the lives of the men of His Church. "Christ has now no other hands but our hands, no other feet but our feet: ours are the eyes with which He looks out compassion on the world." (*St. Teresa*). It is by our daily choices, individual and corporate, that we decide whether the light of the world shall be set on a candlestick or hidden under a bushel. The light is in our hands.

The early Church knew that it was the expression of God's love for men, the instrument for the fulfilling of His purpose on earth. That was almost all about its task that it did know. The few Christians who made up the Church then could not have imagined how they were to preach the Gospel to every creature and they never seem to have discussed it. They knew nothing, and cared nothing, about ultimate targets and workable programmes. To have considered such would only have appalled them. But they did know that they were an instrument in God's hands and that all that mattered was that they should be ready and fit to be used. And they took thought as to the pattern of their life in the Church.

What is the pattern of the Church's life that we see for the future and are trying to achieve in the present? Do we really believe that the Church's life as we know it is likely to serve the purposes of God even as we dimly see them? Has it got the strength of love and the resilience of hope to adjust itself to new conditions and new tasks? Can we envisage any other pattern? Are we trying to create any other pattern?

The future of the Church does not depend on the rightness of our theology nor on our understanding of the contemporary situation. These are, of course, important. But the one essential on which the immediate future of the Church depends is the awareness of its members that they are an instrument in God's hands and their readiness to see that they are fit.

It is, therefore, surely worth while to try to think what

it means to say that the Church is the expression of God's love and the instrument of His purpose in the world and then to see how in its history the Church has shaped itself to be used of God: to ask not so much why the Church was so chosen, which is a question for theology, as to ask how the Church has made itself an instrument, which is a question of history.

We are very apt to think that the Church as we know it is the Church that has always been. Our discussions as to the task of the Church tend to take the Church as we know it for granted. So our discussions are not concerned with what the Church ought to be but with the limits within which the Church can act. Rarely do we ask: " How can the Church be a better instrument ? " Rather we ask, and almost with an air of relief: " What can the Church be expected to do ? "

If we are to see the Church's task with the freedom that comes of knowing that God does not give a task without giving the power, we have, first, to realise that the form of the Church's life has not always been the same as we know to-day. The pattern has been constantly changing. We have, then, to realise that, though human nature may remain much the same, the way that men have lived has also always been changing. We are very apt to think that what we regard as most familiar—our family life, our way of making a living, our relationships with other men in our social groups—has always been much the same and will remain so: that the familiar must be the permanent. And when we feel that these are threatened we think it's the end of our world, for we cannot conceive of a life that is different. And yet these things are constantly changing. The life of a Christian in the first century, the life of a man in Europe in the Middle Ages, the life of one of our ancestors in Reformation Scotland, even the life of our grandparents was essentially different from the life we know and regard as normal, just as the life of a Christian to-day in China or Africa is different from our life. And the difference is precisely in those things that we take as normal and permanent—family life, means of livelihood and social relationships.

If we are not to be paralysed by a fear of change and to be more intent on preserving the fading circumstances of our lives than on meeting Christ in the present, we need to realise that life has always been changing and that the rate of change has never been constant. The change from palaeolithic to neolithic man was slow and centuries of growth were needed to achieve a significant development. The change from Renascence to Industrial man was quick: three centuries saw the way of man's life and the face of the country changed. To-day greater changes are taking place before our eyes. If we can believe the Sunday papers we must be prepared to see the pattern of our life change into new, fantastic, cosmic shapes. For us that is irrelevant, for soon we may read in these same papers articles on a return to a palaeolithic kind of life. Whether we continue to advance by geometric progression or are thrown by our failure to control power into another age of stagnation, the change will not be in the background of our lifes, in a change in the back-cloth of world events, but in the way we live in our homes, in our methods of work and in our relationships with our fellow-men.

And the Church, which is based on the belief that this is God's world and that it is His providence that rules, can never be indifferent to or unaffected by these changes. The Church must ever change with these changes because the essence of love is knowledge. Christ's knowledge of men, which is His love, demands that His Church reveal His love in a creative, resourceful meeting of their needs. And in each age of its history the Church has been able, in so far as Christians have been obedient to that love, to find the form in which it could express that love and could best serve as an instrument of God's purpose.

Naturally the pattern has been constantly changing. And the question is not: "What was wrong with the pattern of the past that is has not remained permanent?" but rather: "Was it adequate for its day and was it used of God?" The proof of its usefulness may well be that it had to pass and give place to another. It may well be that the Church has always failed to be truly an instrument fit for its purpose. It has always been an earthen vessel. That should not surprise us. The wonder is that in each age of revolution the Church did change to a new pattern. That is why we can say that we believe in the Church.

So it is liberating to the mind and encouraging to the heart to look back to the past and to see how the Church was able to adapt itself to a changing present and an unknown future. For that is clearly what must happen to us, or, if not to us, to those who hear God's call. For happen it will. God must find His instrument among men.

But, of course, when we talk of the Church as the instrument of God's purpose, we are not thinking simply of the ecclesiastical organisation of the Church. The essential Church is not its organisation, however necessary that organisation be to preserve continuity. The essential Church is in the lives of men. And the wonder of the Church is that men in the Church, and often quite apart from the ecclesiastical order, have felt called of God to a new kind of life. It is in their obedience that continually the Church has been remade as a living instrument in the hand of God.

This means that we have to look back to the life that men have lived in the Church—which is the real Church history. We have in the past thought too exclusively of Church history in terms of the development of doctrines or of institutions. This is the equivalent of regarding General History as the record of wars and of the development of constitutions. To-day we know that the basis for all history is to be found in the social and economic history of man's life on earth. So we have to begin to try to see how Christian men and women have lived, how they have been affected by the world around them, how far they have succeeded in adapting their lives to the demands of the Gospel and by what means. How was the life of faith first built up among men? How was mission carried out, first in Europe and then throughout the world? It is strange how little we know of that. And yet the fabric of the Church's history is not seen in the books men wrote nor in the resolutions of Assemblies, but in the way men lived and suffered and died.

2. THE NATURE OF THE CHURCH

WHAT is the Church?
In the New Testament we find the Church. It is there already. We can never think of the Christian Faith without the Church. When we think of the Church as an instrument in the hands of God for the fulfilment of His purpose in the world and try to see how the Church in different ages adapted itself to that task, we shall have to think of the Church sociologically rather than theologically. We shall have to ask how men lived in the world and how they behaved in that social organisation called the Church. Naturally we shall have to think of how other men behaved in other groups. But we shall go wrong if we think of the Church as anything but unique. Especially we shall go wrong if we think that there are other groups with which we can compare the Church. We see the power of the idea that the Church is but one among other similar groups in the strange habit that has grown up in recent times of talking about "the Christian Church," as if there were other churches.

There is no other Church, and never has been. There are indeed other religions in the world; and we can compare and contrast what they have in common. And they have much in common: religious buildings, forms of worship, priests, holy books and theological terms. But none of these other religions has anything with which you can compare the Church. And that constitutes a difference so great that it can be claimed that Christianity is something so different that it cannot be called a religion in the same sense in which these are religions: that it is something unique and quite incomparable.

Buddhism, for instance, is certainly a religion. It has temples, priests, holy books, worship and a theology. The one thing it has not got, and does not need, is a body of believers as an essential part of its faith. There are, of course, Buddhists: men who accept its teaching and live their lives in accordance with it. But, unless they become priests, they are merely outsiders, spectators, individual intruders at its services. Buddhism would get along quite happily without them so long as it had its temples and its priests. There have, of course, in recent decades, been attempts to organise these Buddhist believers into various organisations and associations. There is, or was, in China even a Young Men's Buddhist Association. But these are all recent, man-made organisations, human institutions, formed in imitation of what they think is the Church. In the Christian Faith the Church is something intrinsically different. The Faith is the Church and the Church is made up of men and women. In Christianity (and in Judaism and Mohammedanism, for they stem from the same root, and, perhaps we should add, in Communism, for one of its roots is certainly in the Old Testament) places of worship, forms of worship, clergy are all secondary. They are for the well-being of the Church. The Church itself is primary. The Church is the society created by God through Christ. It is into that society that men are called. It is the fact of that society that explains its theology and its work. The most distinctive thing about

Christianity, the thing that marks it off from other religions, is that it is not first of all and in essence a religion but a society of men. The Church is an article of the faith. It is unique.

It is this fact that made the Church a problem to the Roman Empire and that has made it always a problem to the state. The Roman Empire knew how to deal with religion. But a society of men was a different matter. That was a political question. So Christians, then as ever, were not persecuted for religious reasons but because they belonged to a society which made unique claims. They were persecuted for political reasons.

The strange thing is that the early Church, unique as it knew itself to be, never thought of itself as having been founded or as having come into existence at all. The Apostles could not have given a date to the Church's beginning. They would have been quite nonplussed if asked when it was founded. To them it was something quite inevitable, as inevitable to them as God.

Why was this?

We can answer only by going back to what they took for granted, by remembering the faith in which they had been brought up and which Jesus had but confirmed for them—the basic teaching of the Old Testament.

The uniqueness of the Bible as compared with the teaching of the other religions is not that it rests on a belief in God, but that it rests on a belief about God and the world: and not merely on the belief that God is the Creator and Ruler of the world, but on the belief that His Creation is good. The most distinctive sentence in the first chapter of *Genesis* is not the opening statement that: "In the beginning God created the heaven and the earth," but the statement that comes as a refrain after each act of creation: "And God saw that it was good." Most other religions believe that the world owes its existence ultimately to God but, in general, they would hold that that existence is either not truly good or not truly real. Religion for them is a means of rising above the material world or of escaping from it. The Biblical view is quite positive: of essential acceptance rather than of essential denial, God is known through His works and all that He has created is good and therefore has a purpose. The world and life are to be understood in terms of that purpose, which is His purpose. It is not the beginning that matters so much as the goal. Life is to be understood not in terms of origin but of end.

And that belief is not stated only in the first chapter of *Genesis*. There is a sense in which that picture in *Genesis* has, because of its vivid clarity, too much dominated our thinking and made us forget that this belief in the world as God's good creation is as consistently expressed in the prophets and the Psalms and, above all, in Jesus's own teaching. It is the very bed-rock of all the teaching of the Bible. When Jesus says:

> "Behold the fowls of the air: for they sow not, neither do they reap, nor gather into barns, yet your Heavenly Father feedeth them. Are ye not much better than they ? . . . Wherefore, if God so clothe the grass of the field, which to-day is, and to-morrow is cast into the oven, shall He not much more clothe you, O ye of little faith ? . . . Seek ye first the Kingdom of God and His righteousness; and all these things shall be added unto you." (*Matthew* 6, 26-33).

He is saying the same thing as *Genesis* I, but saying it much more vividly and simply, because He is saying what, in all His being, He knows to be true and not, as in the case of the author of *Genesis*, what He wants other men and himself to believe.

And in that passage there is expressed also the second of the Bible's basic beliefs: that God cares for the sparrows, but that man is of much more value to God than many sparrows and that His Kingdom is open to men. We can put that in the more theological language of *Genesis* and say that man is created in the image of God and is alive by His spirit. Thus with a quite unique view of the world—and we should never allow ourselves to forget how surprising it is to say that everything created is good— is linked the equally surprising belief that man is somehow made to be one with God; not in intention only, but in fact; not in some future world but in this. And man knows that, as both *Genesis* and Jesus reveal, in his need of work, in his need to express glory and in his desire for life in fellowship with others.

This faith in the goodness of God's creation and of man's special place in it might well issue in poetic dreaming or in crude despair were it not for the third basic belief of the Bible. It would be a static faith indeed if all that it expressed was that God had created the world and set man in it and the only other fact to be reckoned with was man's failure. But the Bible does not see man's sin as the third great basic belief. The Bible believes in God and not in sin. It sees man's failure as serious and yet not tragic because it holds as the third basic belief that God is all the time at work; that as Creator He is not the engineer who once made the machine in its perfection and left it to deteriorate but the artist Whose hands are ever at work and Whose creation will not be understood until the glory of the end.

This has always been the most difficult thing for men to believe. For it brings God into the here and now. It's comparatively easy to believe that God created the world long ago. At least it's as easy to believe that as to believe anything else. And it's reasonable to believe that, if that is so, He will do something with the world in the end. It's easy to believe in God in the past and in the future— of our own lives as of the world. It's a terrifying thought to believe in God in the present. And yet the only tense for God is the present tense. He is the Lord of the future and of the past because He is the great " I am."

All life's problems arise when we say that we believe in God now, when we say that He is concerned with all life's happenings now as in the past or in the future. For it means that He is concerned with particular events and particular people—all events and all people. The great abstractions lose their meaning. God is not Beauty, Truth and Goodness. He is not the Great Impartial. He is known in His actions. And actions cannot be impartial. To believe in God now is to believe in His actions now, with men and in events. It is to believe that God is at work in man's history.

It is this belief in God the Creator, in Whose image man is made, and Who is ever at work in history, that is the basis of the faith of the Bible; of the New Testament as of the Old; of the New Testament more vividly than of the Old, because more personally.

It is this belief that made the men of the Old Testament know God in the call of Abraham who went out to seek a city and died in hope; that made them see the very proof of their faith in their deliverance out of Egypt. For them God was the Lord Who had brought them our of Egypt: God known in historic fact.

It was this belief that made them into a new community, a society bound to each other and to God by a covenant that was their response to His great act of deliverance. It was because of this belief that they knew that their life together as a people was of infinite importance. It was because God was the Lord Who had led them out of Egypt that they had to find a new faithfulness in the use of their possessions. It was because of this that all who belonged to the community, and even the stranger within the gates, were assured of their place.

It was because of this belief that the prophets arose to recall the people to the basic law of the community. For it was in their failure to hold loyally to their new social life that the people showed their disobedience. Their failure was not in any forgetfulness of their 'religious' practices which all men could understand Their failure was in their disregard of the economic laws that bound them together as a chosen people, in their making of new laws which freed the individual from corporate responsibility. Because the prophets believed that God was the Lord of history they knew that His purpose was ultimately for all men and that the reason why He had chosen some was that His purpose for all might be achieved. It was because of this belief that through tragedy and failure, in times of defeat and of seeming success, and often under the cruellest of conditions, they could live in hope and wait for man's redemption.

And, above all, it was because of this belief that men, some men, were ready to believe in Jesus. For His life and teaching, His death and resurrection would have seemed meaningless without this basic, threefold belief.

The Incarnation would have been incomprehensible unless men had believed that from the beginning God had been in His world at work with men.

And the Church would have been impossible. Without this belief there could have been no Church. It would have appeared as something new, crude and man-made if men had not already believed that this was God's world and had seen His hand at work in their history and now knew, in a way that was strange not in its fact but only in its circumstance and in the wonder of its fulfilment, that what they had long waited for had happened and God had come personally into history in the life and death and resurrection of Jesus.

There was indeed enough that was strange and overwhelming in that. There was the whole manner of its happening in one born to be a carpenter and to die as a criminal. But that was strange only because of their failure to believe that God had already chosen to use them of all people and to realise what that meant for them in love and faith. There was for them the glad shock of realising that all that their fathers had hoped for had come to pass: the shock, almost of anti-climax, of realising that there was nothing to wait for now. But it was not fundamentally strange. It was fulfilment. It was the coming of a great light that lit up the familiar world in which they stumbled. The old was alive now with a new life. They were what they had always longed for. They were, indeed, the new Israel, the society whom God had chosen to use.

And—greatest surprise of all—it had happened, not in some world event too vast for them to understand, but in a Man whose life they had shared. The love of God and His purpose in history were shown to them in One Who had called them by name and had admitted them, through the power of His love, into the fellowship of this new society.

They were His body now, to express His love for men and to be the human instrument of His purposes.

II

THE CHANGING PATTERN OF THE CHURCH'S LIFE

1. IN THE BEGINNING

AND so we have the Church. It had in the beginning no name. It was simply the society of those who believed that in Christ the one thing that mattered had happened, that, through Him and now in their fellowship with Him, God's promises were fulfilled and His purpose was being worked for the world and that they themselves were new men in Him.

We know what they believed and what they preached: that Jesus was alive and at the right hand of God, that He was the Christ through Whom God was bringing in a new age for the world. They called on men to turn and believe and to walk in that new light as they themselves walked. But what is striking in the first chapters of *The Acts* is not the fumbling nature of the words they spoke, but the sureness of the life they lived.

It would seem that quite naturally they went on living the kind of life that they had lived with Jesus on earth; with this difference that, whereas, when they followed Him then, they had not found this way of life natural but had often protested and followed Him sometimes in fear and always in wonder, now they knew that this kind of life was theirs for ever. Then they had had a common purse and depended for their livelihood partly on their own work and partly on the help of their friends. So now they continued to have all things in common. Then Jesus had healed men. So now they healed men in His name.

Then He had broken bread with them and in the breaking of bread had brought them into the secret of His own life. So now they continued in the breaking of bread and found the secret of their life and His still there. For them to believe that He was risen meant firstly and simply that they continued to live the life that He had lived with them and to live it now with freedom and with joy.

It was, in those early days, as if all that was expected of them was that they should continue the kind of life that He had lived with them. As, indeed, it was. Only, of course, it meant a new and ever renewed realisation of what life meant. It meant rapidly widening areas of life even in the first weeks. As numbers grew and opposition increased it meant the facing of new problems. But it was life, not commemoration. It was a new life that they were living in the world and a life that affected all the world, not just a means of commemoration for those who had known Jesus and of imitation for those who had not.

They had to think out what this life meant for them and would mean for others. They had to begin, as we see them doing in *The Acts*, to re-interpret their country's history in the light of what had happened in Christ. They had to find words in which to make the Cross and Resurrection intelligible to men. And so they began to find a theology. Their simple life had to find a more complex form, adequate to their wider contacts and activities. We see this in the development of their worship. It was soon no longer sufficient or possible to go to the Temple to pray. Their own forms of worship had to be built up round " the breaking of bread " but it was still based on the, to them, familiar pattern of the worship of the Synagogue. We see it, too, in the elaboration of the organisation of their common life and from this developed the ministry of the Church. But all this necessary development was subservient to the one fundamental thing that was their task—the living together of the new life that was in Christ.

Theology, worship and the ministry were necessary to help them to live that life and to express to other men their conviction that they were one family called to live that life together. But theology, worship and the ministry were not seen yet as other than secondary.

There were three notes which then were distinctive of this life and which have remained the three notes of the Church to which Christians are at all times recalled and at times forcibly by the crisis of events. Sometimes one or other have been muted and sometimes all three would seem drowned by other noises. But always, and often in quite unexpected quarters, they have sounded out again to recall men to the life that is in Christ.

The first and most important note was simply that Jesus was King of their lives. They were no longer under subjection to the customs of other men. They were a company of men and women who lived as Jesus had taught them to live. They lived under His rule and let His teaching order their lives. What Justin Martyr wrote in the second century applies to the first century as it must apply, even in judgment, to all Christians of any age: " Since our persuasion by the Lord . . . we who valued above all things the acquisition of wealth and possessions now bring what we have into a common stock and communicate to everyone in need; we who hated and destroyed one another, and on account of their different manners would not share the same hearth with men of another tribe, now since the coming of Christ, live on intimate terms with them, and pray for our enemies and endeavour to persuade those who hate us to live according to the good precepts of Christ, so that they may become partakers with us of the same joyful hope."*

The second note was that in the Church there was no distinction of race or class or sex. Perhaps we do not sufficiently marvel that this was so in a tight-knit little

* *Apology of Justin Martyr* I, 14.

community of men of one race, and that the Jewish. Perhaps we have been too much concerned with the problems and difficulties that arose later. We forget that this catholicity was not something the truth of which they learned later through hard experience. They did not learn slowly that men of other races were equally men for whom Christ had died. Rather they struggled against a conviction which they knew that Christ had spoken in their hearts. Likewise they did not come by degrees to the conclusion that women had a place with men in the Church. Rather they consistently tried to diminish the place that women had had in the beginning. In fact there was almost certainly no time in the Church's history when women made a greater contribution than in the first decades of the Church. Even in the New Testament we see their place diminished as we pass from the early writers to the later. For however we interpret the fact that Jesus called no woman to be an apostle—whether we take this as a ruling for all time or assume that Jesus felt that at that time there was no opportunity for women in that work— we must not overlook the fact that women did accompany Jesus and the disciples in their life together and this cannot have been an easier proceeding then than it would be now. Much has been said of Paul's views of the place of women in Church, but no servant of the Church has ever given such generous personal acknowledgement of women as his fellow-labourers. In the last chapter of *Romans* eight women are individually mentioned as working with him. We may be vague as to what form their labour took, but we can certainly assume that their efforts were not employed solely in raising money. The Church found this co-partnership with women difficult and quickly diminished it. Mr. Gardner-Smith has put his finger on a significant point when he shows how the author of the Fourth Gospel " has identified four different women with one another, the nameless woman of Mark, the sinful woman in Galilee,

Mary the sister of Martha, and Mary of Magdala."* It was in Christ that the disciples had known no division.

In terms of class and race there was equally no distinction. This does not mean that there were no difficulties. Masters did not easily forget that they were masters and slaves did not forget that they were men. We see that clearly enough from *Philemon*. But that in Christ there was no distinction was known as truth. From the beginning the right of non-Jews to enter the Church was unquestioned. The controversies that arose were about the terms and methods of their admission.

The third note was that the Church was the foretaste of God's purpose for men. The Church was not in the world to call men to deny the world but to call men into God's purpose for the world. The eschatological nature of the preaching of the early Church, which sometimes makes us to-day think that the Church was then entirely other-worldly, was the index of the Church's conviction that in Christ God's purpose for the world was going to be realised. As Irenaeus put it, the Church was " a completely new oecumenic home intended to receive the peoples of the world and guide them to their destiny beyond all the existing political orders." This new society, however small it was, was still the earnest, the herald and the instrument of the Divine Society which it was God's will to restore among men.

The Church, then, in those early days, was a society of men and women who were seeking to live out the life that had been given them in Christ. It was not enough that they should simply proclaim a gospel to men. It was not enough even that they should convert them to accept that truth. " Christianity," as Canon Alan Richardson says, †" is a religion in search of a social expression." The kind of life that the Church lived was of vital,

* *St. John and the Synoptic Gospels* by P. Gardner-Smith, p. 48.
† *Christian Apologetics* by Alan Richardson, p. 71.

fundamental importance. In Christ its nature and its notes were given to its members. But its form men had still to seek.

2. THE HOUSEHOLD OF FAITH

THOSE early days in which the Church was a small group of people all more or less known to each other did not last long. Very soon it had become a widely scattered society whose members were united to one another not by personal acquaintance but only by a common life and faith.

In the attempt to envisage the life of that society of men of all kinds in all parts of the Roman world, there are two things which are very necessary and very hard for us to appreciate: hard because we can never share their experience and necessary because without an appreciation of them we cannot begin to understand their life and thought. The first is that the Church, then, for the only time in its existence, could not look back on its own history. It was free from the support of a tradition and from its slavery. Jewish Christians could, indeed, look back to the history of their own people but soon they were a small minority in the Church and cut off from their own history. Gentile Christians could find this tradition only in a book which they found hard to read—The Old Testament. It is very difficult for us to understand how vividly they must have felt that they were indeed a new people called to quite a new kind of life. We are often, I think, surprised and disappointed by the naivety and narrow concern of early Christian literature. The reason is to be found, as in the younger Churches to-day, in the overwhelming novelty of the life they are living. And this is probably the reason also why they were so quick to write the history of the facts on which that life was based. For the New Testament enshrined for them the picture of that life to which they were called.

The second thing is that the Church then had no relation, and had no cause to have relation, with the secular world. We are so accustomed to the idea of the Church as having grown as an organic part of society that, unless we know by experience something of the Church on the mission field, we can hardly imagine what it means for a church to be so free and detached. The danger for the Church in that age was that it should forget the secular world, not that it should submit too much to it. That was why Paul had to remind the Christians at Rome, of all places, of their duty to " the powers that be." For Christians, living their own life in the Church and believing it to be a foretaste of the age to come, were only too inclined to think that the business of politics had nothing to do with them. They were apt to forget that the social order had its necessary place in God's purposes.

The Church was apt to forget that because in those first centuries the concern of the Church was to promote among its members the life that was in Christ. In other words, it was with the first of the three notes of the Church that at this period the Church was most particularly, and most naturally, concerned. Not that the other notes were mute. The controversies of the Church in the early days often centred round the problems raised by a society which acknowledged no distinctions of race and class and the preaching of the Church was largely in terms of the new age that God was bringing in. The age that was to come would display in fulness those things that were already evident in the Church through the Resurrection of Christ and the indwelling of the Holy Spirit. And for this reason, and not because it regarded them as indifferent, the Church did nothing about such things as slavery. God had declared the end of all such things and the Church in its own life prophetically knew their end.

To have passed resolutions condemning them would have added nothing at all. But what the Church was from day to day consciously and deliberately concerned with was the up-building within itself of the new life that men had learned in Christ. It was with this that Paul in his letters had been most concerned; and with this he must have been even more concerned in daily living. This prime concern would, naturally, not appear much in the preaching to outsiders and in controversy with unbelievers. And in days when literature was still dominated by the old pre-Christian thinking the side of the Church's work most known to outsiders was inevitably most reflected in the writing of that time. We have always to be careful not to base our views of the life of a society or of part of a society exclusively on contemporary literature. We have to ask first what particular and limited side of life that literature reflects. It is rather from the incidentals and the asides and from the things that happened and also from the quite considerable literature written for reading inside the Church that we can form a picture of the kind of life that Christians lived. And from these it is obvious how largely the Church was concerned with the promotion of the Christian social living of its members.

We see, for instance, the great extent of corporate responsibility for all the troubled lives of Christians. The Church was concerned with the care of the sick, with the care of orphans, with hospitality to fellow-Christians on their travels, with the care of prisoners and of those who had been sent to the mines and with the provision of work for those who were out of work. There was nothing unique or peculiarly Christian in all this care in itself. In the pagan world of that day, as in the China of ours, there were many charitable societies. What was unique was not the care but the nature of the care. That was noticeable to outsiders. It was seen to be different in its very nature. It was not a means of joint insurance against misfortune: it was an expression of love. "See how these Christians love one another," was said originally in seriousness and not in irony. For it was not charitable work by the more fortunate for the less. It arose out of a sense of real community. It had in it something that is reminiscent only of the old Covenant. Its concern for men was not with the accidentals but with the fundamentals of life.

Two of these fundamentals are property and work. And with these the Church's love was vitally concerned. The Church did not accept the world's prevailing views on property. Many Christians felt that the acquiring and holding of private property was theft. Clement, who of all the early fathers has the most to say about property because of them all he was least concerned with controversy with outsiders and most with the inner life of the Church, summed up the Church's teaching when he said: "Christ declares that all possessions are unrighteous when a man possesses them for private advantage, as being entirely his own, and does not bring them into the common stock for those in need."* The Church's view on work was equally definite. The Church regarded work as the duty of every Christian and strongly opposed those who gave up work on accepting the faith. To us that may appear a platitude and strange that men should ever think that work could be avoided by Christians. We forget how far in a pagan society work of any sort ties men to that pagan world and involves them in its demands and customs. The Church refused to allow its members any withdrawal from the daily work of the world. In taking this positive attitude to work, as in taking an avowedly Christian attitude to property, the Church showed itself as a community that ordered its own life in all its aspects according to its own faith and not according to the prevailing customs of the world.

* Quoted in *The Socialist Tradition from Moses to Lenin* by Sir Alexander Gray, p. 48.

The Church did not set out to do general and ameliorative work for outsiders. Such an attitude demands a sense of security and of power alien to a persecuted minority. But what it did offer to men outside was something far more arresting and, to the state, far more dangerous. In the words of Professor Toynbee it offered "a rival civilization of the proletariat." Not that it set out deliberately to do so: but by its life it showed men a society where other values ruled than the power of Rome. By its very language it spoke to men of a community where other things had sway than slavery and money and military might. For words that to us now carry a purely theological meaning had for their early hearers a sense that was far more economic and political. "It is not always recognised how much Christian metaphor comes from a society in which slavery was universal; such words as ransom, Redeemer, 'bought with a price,' freedom, must have made the hearts of those who heard tingle."* And what illuminated these words was the evident fact of a life in which they were real. "Early Christian Churches gave effect to revolutionary ideas in their daily life and practice, abolishing, not only in the dreams of philosophers, but before the eyes of men, the distinction between rich and poor, bond and free, bringing to those who laboured and were heavy laden a different hope."†

It was through its social and economic life, rather than through its preaching and worship, that the Church came into collision with the state. For the Roman Empire could not tolerate within its borders the existence of a great society which lived a life of its own and did things contrary to the teaching of the state, as in the refusal of some of its members to undertake military service, and which gave men hope of another order than the power and discipline of Rome. What Rome feared most of all

* *The Ancient World* by T. R. Glover, p. 346.
† *The Bleak Age* by J. L & B. Hammond, p. 119

was anything that remotely resembled any rival civilization of the proletariat.

What, then, we have in these first three centuries is a Church life quite different from anything of which we in our history in this country have ever had experience. The Church, of necessity, existed apart from and in protest against the ordinary life of men around it. It was a great household of the Faith, a great congregation of congregations scattered over the Roman world. And what was its life ? And how did it spread the Faith ? The word 'congregation' is perhaps misleading. For it was not like anything that we associate with that word. Its unit was not the individual or the family. The Christian family as we know it was then unknown. We see the emergence of the pattern of the Church's life in the greetings that Paul sends to the Church in the home of Priscilla and Aquila at Rome (*Romans 16.5*) and to the Church in the homes of Nymphas and Philemon at Colosse (*Colossians 4.15* and *Philemon 2*). Such gatherings were not drawing-room meetings. The homes of these Christians were probably those of the wealthier Christians in the place. And their households, as most households of the time, were fairly large groups, including slaves and free servants as well as members of the family. We know from Latin writers how much such a household was a social unit. When the household became Christian, it became the meeting place of a much larger group. The group was as large as the home could hold. And so at Colosse there were the two groups. They did not meet only for worship, but for meals. They did not meet only on Sundays, but rather the house was the place of continual gathering all through the week. Travelling Christians found there board and lodging. In a very real sense the Church was the place of living: the centre of the daily life of all the Christians of the place. And it was a home, not a special building set apart for worship.

"The most powerful agency of the Mission during the third century was the Church itself in its entirety."* For the Church under persecution remained this close-knit fellowship, united in common living as in worship and faith. And this, its strength, explains some of its mysteries for us. We do not know the individuals of that Church, as we know the individuals of the later Church. We have few biographies and little biographical detail. That is because the agency of mission was not the individual missionary but the missionary church. In that household of faith men had different gifts but few made of these gifts their profession. The witness of the Church was not the labour of evangelists but of all of the body. We are sometimes surprised how in that early Church so little mention seems to be made of the personality of Jesus. The early Christian writings seem to show a sad declension from the passion and width of the New Testament and to be concerned with such secondary things. But there is no doubt of the simple but not easy love that bound those Christians together: the warm welcome to unknown Christians from elsewhere, the endless hospitality, the care of those in need, the willingness to suffer and even to die. It may well be that the Christian virtues were rather lived than discussed and Jesus was known not in books but in their life together.

So the unit of the Faith was a great family, a household of all types and races, of men and women, Jew and Greek, bond and free. It was scattered, indeed, in countless groups in every province but together it was one household of faith, one in a common belief and one in a strikingly distinctive way of life.

* *The Expansion of Christianity in the First Three Centuries* by Adolf Harnack, translated by J. Moffatt, Vol. I, p. 482.

3. THE MONASTERY

With the recognition of the Church by the state the position of the Church changed and its life with it. From now on the Church and its life are more easily intelligible for us, for the Church is no longer persecuted but exists as an integral part of the general social life of men; in uneasy relationship, indeed, with the state, being used by the state and itself making use of the state, but still accepted and at home. We have thus entered our world, or, at least, the world in which we and the Church of this country have been at home, if not the world in which we and the Church now live. That revolutionary change was not brought about directly by the Church. It may have seemed at the time to be a welcome but not a very revolutionary event. Nothing happened inside the Church. The worship and way of life of Christians was not altered in a night. There was no great change in numbers. The Church had not won its position by becoming a majority. Nor did it cease at once to be a minority. The change was not in numbers nor in any development inside the Church. The change was that the Church gained not only peace but political power and responsibility for the wider life of men.

It's easy for us to look back and say it was a pity. It's easy for us to think of that heroic age of the Church when it knew not power but persecution as the only time when the Church was free to be itself. We forget that what happened must have seemed to Christians then to be the answer of God to the constant prayers of the Church. The Church's destiny is not to be a persecuted minority, though its love must always be willing to endure suffering. The commission of Christ to His Church was to convert the world and His promise that His Church should rule with Him. What that means has always been dark to men. But the evangelistic labour of the Church has always had behind it as the spring of its endurance the apocalyptic hope of that promise. Success in winning men's faith can never be a disappointment to the Church though it may bring profound temptations.

The change had a deep effect on the life of the Church. The bonds, made precious by persecution, that bound men together in the great household of faith became looser when fear went and when the concern of the Church was in terms of wider responsibilities and new duties. This is perhaps best seen in the development of its organisation. The Church ceased to be a world congregation, held together closely by personal links but loosely in organisation, whose natural meeting place was the great representative councils and whose clergy were engaged mainly in the work of building up the internal life of the Church. The clergy found themselves involved more and more in the social and political organisation of the state. Indeed Ambrose and Gregory the Great came to their high office in the Church through high office in the state. The ecclesiastical organisation became increasingly modelled on the civil administration and parallel to it. The result was an organisation on a territorial basis, divided into dioceses and ultimately into parishes. The Church ceased to be an organisation of congregations and councils and tended to become an organisation of officials, with centralisation of authority, as in the state, in Rome. This did not, of course, all happen in a day. But the ecclesiastical organisation was being set in a new shape which was in time to become firm.

The effect of this radical, though gradual, change on the general life of the Church was profound. It may well have seemed at first that Christians could now settle down to a quieter life and a more profitable service. But out of the life of the Church there came a challenge to individuals to assert the original life of the Gospel. Men became acutely aware of the contrast between the teaching of Christ and what Sir Maurice Powicke calls "the still reluctant world,"* and of the need of a more positive and more personal response. This challenge impelled men in two ways: to the desert to a life of aescetic protest and into unknown lands to a life of missionary witness. For if the ease of the times called some to solitary retreat, it called others to a great missionary enterprise. Their achievements were more lasting but less known, for the solitary and the ascetic have always had the better publicity. We often forget that the centuries that followed Constantine were the times of the Church's greatest expansion till the missionary enterprise of the last century.

Both movements were greatly accelerated by the collapse of Rome and by the chaos that followed which put an end to any hope of a life of ease for the Church. The collapse of Rome was the end of the familiar and established order and was therefore a shock to the minds of men, but we probably are wrong if we imagine that it spoke to Christians only in terms of disaster and not of hope. There must have been many Christians among the slaves who streamed out of Rome to welcome the barbarian invaders. "Look to another world," said Columbanus to Boniface. The world-order which men knew and which they had regarded as eternal and as evil was at an end. The present was chaotic and the future quite uncertain. Christians were called to live for another world. " But though the religion of that age was intensely otherworldly, its otherworldliness had a very different character from much that we have come to associate with the word in its modern pictorial form. It was collective, rather than individual, objective rather than subjective, realist rather than idealist. Although the world to come lay outside history and beyond time, it was the final limit towards which time and history were

* *Christian Life in the Middle Ages* by Sir Maurice Powicke, p. 29.

carrying the world."* It was because of that realistic view of the other world and a realistic view of Christ's demands in this that what began in retreat ended in expansion. Men felt called to live according to that other world now.

So one of the most remarkable and effective experiments in Christian living came into being. The monastic movement began as an ascetic and individualistic movement of oriental hermits. It became an experiment in corporate Christian living and the main agent of the age in Christian mission. Augustine in this, as in so much else, put in clear intellectual form what others were feeling and doing. " The Augustininian conception of monasticism was inspired by the ideal of the common life of the primitive Church rather than by the intense asceticism of the monks of the desert."† The monastic movement of the West was deliberately aimed at building up a new type of Christian social living which would permit men in an age of chaos to find the kind of Christian life that men in a more stable society had found in the free household of faith. That is the aim that is common to all the diverse orders that emerged: to Basil and Benedict, to the orders of the Celtic Church and to all the reform movements that arose later. " For St. Basil the social nature of man and the Christian doctrine of the common life of the mystical body proves that the life of a community is necessary to perfection . . . The monastic community was a self-contained society that was completely Christian in so far as it existed only for spiritual ends and was regulated down to the most minute detail by a rule of life which took the place of social custom and secular law."‡

Benedict's Rule became the norm and by far the most influential, not only in his own order but in others. We

* *Christianity and the Rise of Western Culture* by Christopher Dawson. p. 36. † *Ibid*, p. 50.—‡ *Ibid*, p. 50.

see from it how, in establishing " a school of the Lord's service, in which we hope to order nothing that is harsh or rigorous,"* he was experimenting with a new kind of life for men. The first principle of it was that it existed for the praise of God. It was a social life in which individuals came together to find a kind of life now altogether unobtainable outside, where they could try seriously to obey the demands of Christ. The attraction of that life rather than any rigour of self-denial shines through Benedict's Rule. The second principle is tacitly assumed rather than explicitly stated. The new society was not a clerical society. It was at first essentially for lay people, or rather it was for ordinary Christians, for the rigid distinction between clerical and lay had not yet been drawn. It was the success of the movement and the need of some kind of corporate life for the clergy that soon made the combination of the monastic life with the priesthood so common. But in origin it was not a movement for the clergy. And this fact probably lies behind the constant struggle throughout the Middle Ages between the monastic orders and the territorial or secular clergy. The original monks were not priests. It is laid down in the Rule that if an abbot wants to have a monk ordained for the services of his monastery he may choose from among his monks one who was worthy of ordination.† Ordinary men who, because of the turmoil of the times and the breakdown of ordinary social life, found it hard to live as Christians and perhaps hard to live at all found in the monastery a place where there was security and fellowship and work: a society which was quite different from the world of conflict and autocracy outside, for in the monastery there was the dignity of equality and even the Abbot held rule only by the election of his fellows.

And so the third principle of the monastery was that

* *Prologue to the Rule of St. Benedict.*
† *Rule of St. Benedict,* Chapter 62.

it was a social life in which work—manual work—had an integral place. This work was seen not only as necessary for a man's spiritual life but as necessary also for the life of the community, if it was to be truly 'a school of the Lord's service.' And this insistence on work was as revolutionary as the conception of the social life of the monastery. " The Benedictine Abbey was a self-contained economic organism, like the villa of a Roman landlord, save that the monks were themselves the workers and the old classical contrast between servile work and free leisure no longer obtained."*

And the fourth principle was that the life of the monastery must be based on a time-table. It is only by a time-table that you can break down old customs and forms of action and impress on men's lives a new pattern. And it was to that time-table, which regulated work and meals and leisure, that the worship of God—the main activity of this life—was tied.

It is important for us to appreciate how deliberate an innovation all this was and how carefully it was planned down to its smallest detail. The attraction to men—and to women—was that it offered a new and ordered way of life utterly different from the disturbed life of a fearful society. It gave to them work and security and a meaning to their lives in a world where all was turmoil and uncertainty. We can feel that attraction in the words put by Aelred of Rievaulx in the mouth of a novice in the great days of the expansion of the Benedictines in Britain. We may call it an ideal picture but need not doubt the sincerity of its attraction. " No quarrels, no contentions, no complaint and lamentations of the peasant for his dire oppression; no lamentable cry of the injured poor; no pleas at law or judgments in the Courts. Everything is peace and quiet, and a marvellous freedom from worldly

* *Christianity and the Rise of Western Culture* by Christopher Dawson, p. 51.

tumults. Such is the unity and concord among the brethren, that each thing seems to be all men's, and all things each man's. And what doth marvellously please me, here is no acceptance of person, no consideration of birth."*
What men gave up in taking the vows of poverty, obedience and celibacy was offset by what they gained in a life of security, fellowship and peace. But it was only the discipline of a time-table and the conviction of a call to find a new pattern of active Christian living that made the movement effective. When these were gone neither vows nor attraction could make it live.

The effect of this movement on the economic and cultural life of the West has always been recognised. The monasteries preserved learning. They, at least in the beginning, gave education. And, as important as anything, they maintained and developed agriculture. These were the inevitable consequences of the development of a new stable form of social living. But these were not the aims of the monastic movement: they were incidental to its progress. The movement was not based on such thoughts of economic planning. Rather it arose out of the determination of men to preserve the life of the Church and to extend the area of the Faith. It is noteworthy that men, like Gregory, who felt the call to aggressive missionary work, found membership of a monastic community essential. The monastic movement was the only means available at the time for securing the resources necessary for missionary work and for maintaining its continuity. Without it, it is scarcely conceivable that Europe would have been evangelized. In the old Roman world the evangelistic mission of the Church had been carried out by the witness of the Christian community rather than by the labour of professional missionaries. " Between A.D. 500 and A.D. 1500 men who gave up the major part of their time to

* Quoted in *Scottish Abbeys and Social Life* by G. G. Coulton, p. 42.

propagating their faith had a much larger share in the expansion of Christianity than in the days when the Graeco-Roman world was being won."* This was inevitable when the Church moved out into a disturbed world and into non-Christian lands and it would have been impossible if the monasteries had not been there to produce the men and to support them. Britain owed its faith to two monastic movements: " the Irish community at Iona and the Roman mission at Canterbury: both were monastic."† And it was to monks from Britain that the conversion of Northern Europe was largely due. Indeed, at this time, Northern Europe was the scene of the Church's expansion because of the development of Western monasticism: Eastern Europe was the scene of its withdrawal because there monasticism remained individualistic.

So we find at a time of social and political disintegration the development within the Church of a new form of Christian social living to meet the needs of the time. It was spontaneous in that men welcomed it for what it gave them of an individual life of faith. But it was deliberate in that some men saw clearly that the old pattern of the Church's life was doomed and that a consciously planned pattern of life could alone preserve the faith.

It was very different from the form of Christian life in the previous period. No longer was it possible to have a great household of the faith, close-knit in personal links but loose in organisation, existing over against a different world outside. Something much more organised could alone survive and do the work of mission. The new unit had to be created and it was made up of individuals and not of households. The convent was composed of

* *A History of the Expansion of Christianity* by K. S. Latourette, Vol. II, p. 9.

† *Church Life in England in the Thirteenth Century* by J. R. H. Moorman, p. 2.

individuals—men and women—who deliberately and individually chose a corporate way of life. The consequence of this new conception of Christian living was far-reaching.

Of course, it was only a minority in the Church who chose this way. The rest of men and women went on living their lives as well as they could in a changing world. But the presence and the example of the monasteries were of immeasurable help to them, in setting before them an example of positive Christian living and in affording them practical help in education and training. The vows of poverty, obedience and celibacy were what divided the monks from ordinary men. But they had a profound influence on the lives of ordinary men. The vow of poverty meant not destitution but security and kept before men the idea of corporate property. The vow of obedience did not mean for the monk a blind obedience to authority but recognition of his place in a purposeful community. It gave him status and brought him responsibilities. It was obedience within a responsible community in which he had his place. This idea affected the thinking of men about ordinary social life for centuries to come. The vow of celibacy, for all its dangers as a doctrine, was perhaps needed as a fact, to preserve the idea of the task of the Church's Mission and to emphasise the individual's responsibility in dedication.

It has always been through the minority who have been willing to make experiment that new life has come to the Church.

4. CHRISTENDOM

THE MIDDLE AGES (A.D. 1000-1500) are a very difficult period for us to see clearly. There is so much to see and it is so conflicting and various. There is a freshness—and a starkness—about the Dark Ages which makes its happenings clear. For all our lack of detailed information, or perhaps because of it, we can imagine more easily the kind of life men lived and what they were doing in the five hundred years before A.D. 1000 than in the five hundred years after. The great men seem simple and heroic. That is partly because we see them against a background that is grim and austere and partly because the issues they faced were simple. And against that blankness of ordinary life the monasteries stand out clearly in their work, their achievement and their glory.

There is nothing of that drabness in the five hundred years that follow. It is a scene of colour and movement and conflicting achievements, in which the great figures are of more subtle personality. There has been in the past a tendency to invest the mediaeval period with too simple a social pattern by the use of such words as feudalism and chivalry. Perhaps to-day we see it in too simple an intellectual pattern. We forget that those patterns are not pictures of what society actually was but are rather theories of what men would have liked society to have been. That is why they appear at the end and not at the beginning of a period. It is when men know that the certainty of a hope is gone that they put that hope down on paper as a belief. Such theories are no sure guide to what was actually happening, but only to what some men wanted to believe. We forget, also, that not only did Aquinas come towards the end of our period, but that his teaching was not generally accepted till later. Men declared a unity that was lost even as we to-day look back to the idea of Christendom with a nostalgic interest.

And yet, despite the fact that the Middle Ages were a time of great changes and of conflicting developments, Christendom was a new reality. Christendom may have been more a faith than a fact. Yet it was a faith. Men felt that they belonged to a unified society, rooted in the one faith. This gave to them a sense of community and a pattern of life; a generally accepted code of morals and the idea of a supreme authority. Thus each man felt that he had a place in that society and was content. For even if through misfortune you lose your place, or even if it is a very miserable place, the comfort of knowing that society has a place for you is very different from the despair of knowing that society has no place at all for you.

And this applied to men everywhere in Christendom. This was something quite new. It would have been inconceivable in the early centuries when 'the world' was outside the Church and unattainable in the Dark Ages when all was conflict. The world to which this applied was, indeed, a small world, contracted further by Moslem invasion, but within its borders there was the acceptance of the conviction that society was one, that church and state were complementary and that each man had his place. That was a social order that the world had not known before and has not known since. And it was the monasteries of the previous age that had made Christendom possible. The monasteries not only, by their preservation of the Christian life, enabled Christendom to emerge, they also set the pattern for the new conception of social life that held Christendom together. That conception was of the 'religious' life. And 'religious' meant not simply 'belonging to the faith' but 'belonging to an order.' But the idea of an 'order' was very wide. It had a place for the soldier as well as for the saint. It had a place, and a very great place, for women. In no age since the first decades of the early Church had women been given so large and important a place in the life of the Church. Women as well as men had their recognised place in the religious life: their opportunities for devotion, for charity and for a life of action.

But it was a 'religious' scheme of life. The secular world, for all the theory of a place for every man, was outside that scheme, more definitely outside than it had been in the Dark Ages. The men and women who did not enter an order were increasingly left alone. And they were becoming more conscious of their own lives and more aware of their own desires. The pattern of all the Church's life was now affected by the pattern of monastic life. Celibacy now became the rule for all the clergy. The worship of the Church became increasingly that of the monastic community rather than of ordinary life. And that 'religious' pattern was itself becoming more and more individualistic. "The piety of the Middle Ages was largely individualistic."* As it was the individual who entered the monastery, so it was an individualistic conception of worship that developed. The great corporate and realistic conception of the 'other' world changed to and individualistic and subjective conception. The great pictures of the triumphant Christ so often painted on the walls of early Churches, the symbol of that eternal world which is the goal of this, gave place to the crucifix in an individual's hands. "The earliest crucifixes show Him robed and crowned, the Victor reigning from the Tree: but gradually the crucifixion descends from heaven to earth, till finally the eyes of Christ are closed in death, and we see the realistic picture of human suffering."† The 'other' world had come to mean a world to which the individual escapes from this world of misery.

And so the idea of the Church as the home of men in this world became an anachronism, just at the time when in theory all had their place in it. The secular clergy held their importance because of their territorial position and not because of their pastoral function. More and more parishes passed into the patronage of the monasteries who regarded them not as fields of service but as estates to maintain their religious life. The ordinary life of men was less and less considered.

What ordinary men and women—peasants and yeomen,

* *Liturgy and Society* by A. G. Hebert, p. 112.
† *Liturgy and Society* by A. G. Hebert, p. 83.

merchants and squires, wives and mothers—got from the Church was now very little: very much less than in the Dark Ages. They had now no participation in the worship of the Church. There were no hymns or singing. There were no Bibles in many churches. The sermon had dropped out. We must remember that there was " no example of pulpits in England earlier than about 1340."* In the fourteenth century, Pecham, the first Franciscan Archbishop of Canterbury, made a revolutionary move when he demanded that his clergy should preach at least four times a year. The services in the churches were conducted with little dignity or reverence. We read of churches used for fairs and markets, as breweries or as store-houses for corn.† The people communicated but rarely, usually once a year, at Easter, and then only in one kind. This custom of receiving the bread alone did not originate until the twelfth century and was symptomatic of the decreasing concern of the Church with the life of the laity.

The ordinary life of men, in family, at market and in the fields, was less and less touched by the Church. And this was happening as ordinary men were becoming more conscious of themselves and more aware of the importance of their own affairs. For in these centuries new life was stirring and the movements of that new life affected the ' lay ' rather than the ' religious.'

It was through the Church's failure to adapt itself to what was happening in these new movements that Christendom broke down. For these new movements were due to developments in the economic, the cultural, and the political life of men and a Church order that denied or disregarded them was doomed.

In the range of men's economic life great changes were

---

* *Preaching in Mediaeval England* by G. R. Owst, p. 161.
† *Church Life in England in the Thirteenth Century* by J. R. H. Moorman, p. 148.

taking place. We can see the change perhaps most clearly in the development of the monastic movement itself and that development indicates how a form of Christian social living adapted to one period of history may fail utterly in the next. The monastic movement had started as an essentially lay movement: it had become the very epitome of the ' religious.' It had started as an experiment to recover the simplicity of the life of the primitive Church: it ended by becoming the pioneer of capitalism. " Capitalism was, in fact, the great heresy of the Middle Ages: the chief challenge to the ideal claims of Christianity."* Through their very success in attracting men and gifts, through their work and their continuity, unaffected by death or inheritance, the monasteries had become part, and a major part, of the land-owning class. The monks were practically the pioneers in estate management and in new methods of farming. This was especially true of the Benedictines. " Their scattered estates were treated as a single administrative ' bloc ' and were commercialised."† The Cistercians, who had settled in the more remote and less inhabited areas in order to get back to the simple life, were, though not the originators, the great developers of the wool trade. " They were the first to develop sheep-farming for the export market on a really large scale and they, together with the other new orders who imitated their economy and settled in the same districts, remained, at least until the fourteenth century, the most powerful group of wool growers and the producers of the finest fleeces."‡ This led to interests outside their direct husbandry: to their participation in commerce and finance. " The larger abbeys of white monks and canons in the North naturally attracted to themselves as focal points all the wool of the

---

* *The Condition of Man* by Lewis Mumford, p. 159.
†*The Religious Orders in England* by Dom David Knowles, p. 51.
‡ *Ibid*, p. 51.

neighbourhood and there is early evidence that conversi*
were sent round to gather it in. This traffic, which was
in direct contradiction to the spirit of Citeaux, was
expressly forbidden by General Chapter, but it was the
common practice all over England and far too lucrative
to be dropped."† Thus the monasteries, perhaps more than
other sections of society, laid the foundation for the rise
of Capitalism.

So the monastic movement, which had originated in a
community of ordinary men united in prayer and work,
became a religious order owning large property and
indulging in trade and finance. The monks ceased to work,
except in the management of their estates. The lay brothers
gave place to servants.

And this change in the life of the religious orders was
paralleled by a new teaching about work. The Church
now nourished the idea of the accumulation of wealth
and taught men to work " not first for a living but for the
sake of accumulation of wealth which would lead to a
further production of wealth."

But this development and teaching, which the Church
did so much to promote, led to the emergence of new
social classes outside the old recognised order of society.
It led to the rise of cities always at loggerheads with
feudal society and to the growth of the power of merchants
and bankers. And, at the other end of the scale, it led
also to the emergence of a new class of landless and dispossessed men, equally outside the old society. And in
both these new classes was the consciousness of needs
and aspirations unrecognised by Christendom.

In the range of culture, too, changes were taking place.
There was a general stirring of a new intellectual life.
We see it in the rise of the universities, in the birth of
popular and sometimes pagan song, as in the Troubadours,

* Servants.
†*The Religious Orders in England* by Dom David Knowles, p. 68.

and in new forms of art. And, though inevitably most of the pioneers of the new learning were clerics, the area of this new cultural activity was outside the ordinary bounds of the religious life. The universities were the creations of Church officials and owed much to the teaching of the Friars but, in essence, they belonged to the secular world. The subject matter of art was no longer theological. The topic might be Biblical but the treatment reflected the life of the town and the home rather than that of the Church and the convent. And of that art the prince and the merchant were the patrons rather than the Bishop and the Abbot.

And thirdly, in the range of political life, the rise of national monarchies broke the unity of men's social thinking and made them think more in terms of their secular relationships, of class and trade and nation, than in terms of a ' religious ' community.

So, while the Church was giving less and less thought to laymen's lives, laymen were acquiring a new self-consciousness and were learning to think for themselves.

That is why Francis is so important a figure and why he has aroused the imagination and affection of men of all traditions from that day to this. That is also why he stands by himself and not for what he achieved. In him we see the new movements finding expression and a new answer. In his followers in the order that bore his name but little more of his, we see the failure of the Church and the reason why Christendom was at an end. " What St. Francis desired was not a new religious order nor any form of ecclesiastical organisation but the following of Christ—a new life which would shake off the encumbrance of tradition and organisation and property and learning and recover an immediate personal contact with the divine source of life, as revealed in the Gospel."* His original

* *Christianity and the Rise of Western Culture* by Christopher **Dawson**, p. 257.

followers were laymen who adopted nothing of the conventional religious life of the time. They were a living protest against all that. Of the eight Franciscans who first landed in England, only one was ordained and he was not the leader. They went into the common ways of men: into the cities, into the markets, into the universities. They preached in the language of the people and spoke with fervour and passion and even with the beauty and tricks of the Troubadour and mountebank. Their appeal was especially to the new classes that the new Capitalism had called into being: to the new men of the towns, the merchants and the bankers and the dispossessed, and their great recruiting ground was the university.

Francis was unique, but in all he did he was very much the son of his time. What he felt so intensely was what others felt dimly. What he sought to do through popular preaching and the life of poverty was what had been already expressed in the heresies—the Waldensians, the Albigenses, and the Lollards. For these heretical movements "were marked by an attempt to lead the apostolic life: that is to say, the life of poverty and preaching."* The Friars—Dominicans and Franciscans—were recognised as orthodox but that should not blind us to the fact that they were, in origin and intention, revolutionary.

The Franciscan order failed of Francis's original intention. But that is not to say that Francis failed for he sought no organisation. He saw his brotherhood as a body of men who simply did the Lord's work. He would gladly have left it at that and had no thought for the future. He saw no need either of order or of orders. But when men decided to carry on his work, they brought into existence an autocratic authority and an organisation that spelt the end of Francis's spirit. The Franciscan order became clerical. Within a hundred years it was in no sense different from the older orders against which

* *The Early Dominicans* by R. F. Bennett, p. 7.

Francis had protested. It became famed for its learning. It gave up work. It owned property.

Why was this declension? It was surely because the followers of Francis could not see anything else to do. In the turmoil of the emerging new society they were not able or were not forced by circumstance, to find a new pattern of Christian social living. The old tradition of the religious life was still too strong for them or the new forms of life were still too weak to constitute an area in which to create a new life. Perhaps Francis had hoped that out of the experience of the simple life to which he led men some new pattern would emerge. More probably he had the strength never to hope and was content to leave it to the future. Certainly he knew in his heart that the organisation that his followers wanted, based as it was not on their experience of this new life but on the old life that they saw around them, could not achieve anything. So, to their perplexity, he refused to have part in their organisation. Men had to learn to be fools first. Men had to keep charity with the poor before they could begin to think of a new society. They had to break down for themselves the walls that Francis for himself had pierced and passed through. But instead they repaired the walls—of organisation, of property and of learning. And men had to wait, as Francis probably knew they would have to wait. So he remains not the founder of an order but the prophet for men of all types of the need to get back to the simplicity of Christ.

So at the end of the Middle Ages, during which the idea of Christendom had been a great reality, the Church was left without a pattern in which to express the Faith in a world which was rapidly changing. The idea of Christendom had been that of a community in which each man had his place and therefore his dignity and in which the various orders of the community were linked to those above and below through obedience and responsibility. Christian life was lived by ordinary men and women in terms of that one community and their ordinary avocations were seen as serving their function in it. " The Christian idea had been capable of creating an ever-growing community which, in the shape given to it by the Mediaeval Church, had become a power great in intensity as well as extent . . . But now in a society with a heightened consciousness of the self and of property, matters of the mind too were affected by the idea of private property, bringing with it egoism and personal feelings, jealousy and rancour."* The Church had created the community but it had allowed the three notes of its original being to be muted. It, indeed, still made no real distinction of race or class or sex but it had accepted a fatal new distinction which broke through the whole of life—the distinction between clerical and lay, between religious and secular. The Church could not be said to be living the life that was in Christ when the organised Church lived detached on its own wealth. By its emphasis on an individualistic piety it betrayed the hope of a new oecumenic home for all men. Well might Francis feel that Christians had to get back to the love of Christ.

5. THE CHRISTIAN FAMILY

"Down to 1500 the family was without Christian ritual."† That is certainly true of the centuries we call the Middle Ages. In the earliest centuries there was almost certainly Christian ritual in the Christian households of the Roman Empire, for these were the first Churches, and in the Dark Ages the Church had its place and its teaching in the families of its members. But in the Middle Ages the Church had more and more left

* *Sociology of the Renaissance* by Alfred von Martin, pp. 30, 31.
† *The Christian Future* by E. Rosenstock-Huesy, p. 36.

the ordinary life of men alone, and Christian ritual had faded away outside the 'religious life.' We see this in the constant, unsuccessful attempts of the Church to enforce marriage as a religious ceremony in Church, or even at the Church door. This, of course, was the inevitable consequence of making a sharp distinction between the religious and the secular life and of making the religious life a celibate life. The home life of men was left almost entirely secular. The Christian family could not be said to exist. All that there was was the natural family existing in a Christian community.

What made the Reformation possible, what made some kind of reformation inevitable, was that by 1500 something had begun to happen to change the idea of the family. This was the beginning of one of the greatest of silent revolutions. We see it reflected in the way in which monkish chronicles give place to family letters and domestic records. It is only now that we of to-day could conceivably begin to feel ourselves at home in men's houses. It was due partly to the greater security of life. Defence was no longer the overwhelming consideration in architecture. The manor house had ousted the castle. Domestic architecture began to rule. It was due partly to education. Learning was no longer the preserve of the clergy. A married man need no longer be illiterate. Largely it was due to the economic, cultural and political changes mentioned in the last section. Men—not, of course, all men, but those who now had a certain security of power and knowledge—began to assert their right to a place in society and to make for themselves a pretty large place. And that place was not made by the creation of any new 'order,' to enter which they would as individuals have had to withdraw from ordinary life. That place was in their homes, in the life that they shared with their families. The strangely modern and vividly captivating picture of the home life of Sir Thomas More was typical of what was beginning to happen in the sixteenth century. It could not have existed earlier.

We can trace the causes of the Reformation in the economic, social and ecclesiastical developments of the previous centuries. But the Reformation would never have been anything but an ecclesiastical movement if this new emergence of the family had not given it a new area of social living in which to develop. The doctrinal controversies round which the Reformation turned would easily have become but greater discussions in the schools if passion had not entered to give conviction and a purpose and a feeling of new life. And that passion came from the demand of these men for a greater scope for their lives and for a fuller expression of their faith in their homes. That was why the Reformers found most response in the towns, among merchants and in the universities and least response where these new forces were least in evidence.

It was their belief that the Faith was concerned with the ordinary life of man and the desire to make it find its centre in the family that united the Reformers, so diverse otherwise in their theological opinions. And this, as much as their theology, was the basis of their piety. Luther made his abiding impression on German life by his theology but perhaps even more by his new picture of the Christian home. It was that more than anything else that set its peculiar stamp on Lutheran piety. Calvin, with a different pattern that issued in a different piety, gave the family a basic place in the Christian life and the influence of this teaching was probably more lasting there than in the sphere of politics.

And this emphasis on the family as the new unit of Christian living was not confined to Protestants. They had not called the new family into being. They had found it and were, indeed, the products of its emergence. They saw its significance and gave it a theology. So also did the Roman Church. Through the Counter-Reformation equally, if in a different way, it made the family now the basis of its piety. The Holy Family—but only after the Reformation—became the picture of Christian living for ordinary men and women in the Roman Church. Such a picture was unknown in the Mediaeval Church. The Virgin Mary had been the great intermediary for individuals. The new worship of Mary and reverence for Joseph meant that religion had to do again with the family life of men and women.

But it is with the Reformers that we are most concerned. The Reformation expressed itself in the destruction of images and of everything that made a division between the religious and the secular life, in the substitution of the Common Table for the Altar, in the participation of all believers equally in the bread and wine, in the demand that the Bible and all worship be in the language of the people, in the insistence on preaching and teaching, in the encouragement of education and in the enforcement of a Christian ritual in the home as well as in church. The exaggeration and the ruthlessness of the Reformers cannot be understood unless we appreciate the object of their passion. The devotion of ordinary men and women and the strength of the new piety cannot be understood unless we see how much this passion meant for them.

That devotion and that piety were centred on the family. The Church was no longer thought of as the only place for worship, or even as the main place of worship. That, as much as fear of Romish practices, was the reason for the decay of worship in the Church and the lack of interest in Church architecture. Men no longer built Cathedrals: they built stately homes. The home, not the Church, was the centre of life. The home, and not the Church, was the place of daily prayer. The Church was the place of teaching and soon preaching almost obliterated all else. Just as the founders of the monastic movement deliberately set up a new pattern of daily life in the monasteries, with its rigid time-table of daily prayer and work, so the Reformers with equal deliberation laid down the pattern of daily family life which they saw now as the basis of Christian living. And both—Monks and Reformers alike—in concentration on their new experiment had to break with and deny the old. " Every family now was cemented into a spiritual unit while before it was purely hereditary and economic. By the reading of Scripture, by the singing of hymns, the common prayer at meals in the native tongue, in the homes of lay families, their homes gained a new power."* That word ' every ' may seem to us to-day an exaggeration. But it was then no matter of individual choice. The new discipline of family life was enforced with all the authority of Church and State. Most welcomed it gladly for it must have seemed the law of their inheritance. Even the hypocrites never doubted the need.

For it was the family that made the new society. It was in the family that men could find the strength to withstand the old tyrannies of an effete order and could build a new life for themselves and their children. The family, rather than the estate or manor or guild, became the unit of economic life. And behind this new development, sustaining it and giving it its intellectual basis, were the great beliefs of the Reformation—the Sovereignty of God, Justification by Faith and the Priesthood of all believers. These were living and powerful beliefs because they were clothed in the stuff of common life. The belief in the Sovereignty of God took the place of the early Church's belief in an ' other ' world which was the end of this, and of the mediaeval Church's vision of Heaven or Hell for the individual. It had that apocalyptic quality without which religion can have no passion and no power. God was the Ruler of the world now and all men were called to His service in all the activities of their lives—in their

* *The Christian Future* by E. Rosenstock-Huesy, p. 36.

daily occupations as much as in their religious activities, in their homes as much as in Church. It was an apocalyptic of the present rather than of the future, and its abuses were those of men who had no time for hope.

This was a revolutionary change in the pattern of Church life. With the family the basis of Christian living, the Church ceased to be a company of individuals at worship, as it had been in the Middle Ages, and yet was something different from the household of faith of the early centuries. It was essentially a community of families. In Northern Ireland we see the strength of this tradition in the custom that still remains of counting the membership of a congregation not, as now in Scotland, by the number of individual communicants but by the number of families, all of whose members may not be communicants.

It was this concentration on the family that offset the greatest failure of the Reformers. For it is not too much to say that the Reformers denied utterly the essential note that the Church is a society without distinction of sex. They broke down the barrier between religious and lay but they erected another barrier between men and women. They gave women less of a place than in the Middle Ages for they gave her none. In Mediaeval times there had been a very definite place for women in the religious life. Their right to it was recognised to be as valid as the right of men. That place disappeared with the dissolution of the convents. No other place was made for them. Monks could be and were absorbed in the regular ministry but where could women go? For men the ministry remained and there was a new order of service for laymen in the eldership. But no opportunity either of a specifically religious vocation or of service in the Church was offered to women. The Reformed Churches were exclusively masculine in their actions and their teaching. Women were regarded purely functionally as wives and mothers and were too often treated as the agents of man's fall. Men are regarded as by nature called to rule and their conception of rule was more often the Judaistic idea of enforcing obedience than the Christian idea of serving in love.

Woman's place was in the home. But because the home was the new unit of Christian and of social living women came to win for themselves in that domestic field a new place and a new scope. In the three centuries that followed women came to occupy a more and more prominent place in society but always, as it were, in a private capacity. They exerted a tremendous influence but always in silent opposition. Their place in the philanthropic movements of the nineteenth century is very significant. Elizabeth Fry and Florence Nightingale could never have done what they did if women had not become persons in their homes and learned the use of silent power.

The father was the high-priest in the family. The doctrine of vocation gave him that position, for vocation was thought of only in terms of men. He was called to serve the will of God in his daily life; in his home and in his work. No longer had men to enter the 'religious' life to serve God. God's call was to baker and farmer, teacher and king as much as to minister. This doctrine gave to men an energetic activity that would bring the business of the world under God's rule and purpose. It made them autocratic in their homes.

The Calvinist idea of vocation was in theory little different from the mediaeval idea of ordered status.* It was expounded in protest against covetousness and ambition. The burden of early Puritan preaching was that men should be content in their calling. By the eighteenth century the emphasis had changed, to the prudential conception of calling. It meant now that individuals had different aptitudes and each should be

* See *Aspects of the Rise of Economic Individualism* by H. M. Robertson, pp. 8-16.

allowed to develop them in competition with others to the best of his ability. From being mediaeval in its conception of a community in which each man's vocation fitted in to form a whole it became mercantilist in its belief in free trade, competition, and private property. But the freedom that men sought was not, in their minds, freedom from the Church but freedom from state control. And the Church, often, was on their side.

This new conception of the obedience of Christian men demanded the creation of a whole new scheme of virtues: not of the cloister but of the world, not the virtues that opened the way to the eternal hereafter but the virtues that make men obedient to God in this life. It was a tremendous task and perhaps it is not surprising that it was never accomplished. The theory was there in Calvin but its working out in practice was incomplete. It was fairly adequately worked out in the sphere of the family. The domestic virtues were specified and inculcated. And it is these that have given strength and its peculiar character to our tradition: integrity, truthfulness, consideration for the weak, courtesy. The Christian man was the man whose home was Christian, who was upright in his conduct with outsiders and considerate of the unfortunate with whom he came into personal touch. The failure of the Reformed Church was that it stopped there. It did not proceed to a like reinterpretation of the virtues of political life or to a new formulation of the virtues of commercial and industrial life. Commerce and industry developed too quickly: they lacked the stability of the family. All that was, in the end, expected of men was that they should carry the domestic virtues—kindness, temperance, honesty—into their personal relations with those with whom they had to do outside their homes. It was not expected that these virtues should become the basis of the economic system. The aim and methods of trade were left unquestioned. This was not part of the

Reformers' intention, least of all of Calvin's, but the refusal of their successors to go further in their interpretation of Christian ethics meant that they accepted the idea of economic individualism and let it develop. In the end they accepted the later mediaeval Church's attitude to the making of money. Indeed the doctrine of vocation, as later interpreted, gave an added sanction to the accumulation of wealth. Economic progress and moral elevation were considered as synonymous. This and the worship of thrift encouraged a greater accumulation of wealth. The domestic virtues were kept outside the door behind which money was made. And soon it was not proper for a man to talk ' shop ' at home. The place of work and the place of family life were divided. The world of business and not the teaching of Christ decided wherein success lay. " Success in a man's secular vocation was too often wrongly considered as a confirmation of his election and consequently too often property and wealth have been treated as an index of a man's true worth or a nation's standing in the sight of God. Calvinism did not hold aloof from affairs as Romanism and even Lutheranism did, but accepted ' business ' as the appointed sphere for the testing and strengthening of souls. Ambition was consecrated by obtaining a religious sanction and became a motive worthy of being sublimated into a sense of vocation and many of the best and some of the worst things in modern life are the result."*

The results were to appear in this tragic form later. The mediaeval Church had had its doctrine of obedience, by which men knew their place in the community. It had its model in the monastic vow of obedience, which was obedience within a fellowship. The Reformed Church as it developed found no equivalent for this obedience.

* *Protestant Ethic and the Spirit of Capitalism* by W. R. Forrester (*Expository Times*, September, 1937).

It was concerned most with those who had made good and allowed them to be obedient to their success. Those who worked for others could interpret obedience only as obedience to their masters. The idea of obedience in a Christian community gave place to the idea that the virtue required of those who had was to assert themselves and get on, and the virtue of those who had not was to be docile. But so long as society was essentially rural the dangers of these divided ethics were hidden by the strength of the family and by the fact that the place of living and the place of working could not be separated. For the essential unit of the Reformation family was the home of the farmer or the peasant or the home of the merchant in his small town, just as the parish of the Reformed Church was essentially the rural parish or the small town. There the home was the centre of the family's work and the unit was larger than the narrow blood relationship of father and son. Those who shared in the family work shared in the family life. Children were brought up knowing about and sharing in the work of their elders and in contact with varied generations. That was the typical family life before the Industrial Revolution. We see it reflected in biographies, diaries, novels and family histories. It is still very largely the picture that is in our minds when we speak of the Christian family. That is where our inherited teaching about the family finds its proper setting. And when stories to-day are written for or about children we have to get them back to such a setting even to tell a story. We do that because the roots of all our thinking about the family are still there.

So long as rural life remained the formative pattern of ordinary life the tragic failure of Christian thinking to rule the world of business was not apparent. At least the Church, firmly embedded in that life and sure of its rule over men in their homes, did not see the division it had left to widen. It was the economic thinkers and the philosophers who made the division clear and gave to men in business their right to freedom in their own affairs. Locke wrote: "The Church itself is a thing absolutely separate and distinct from the commonwealth. The boundaries on both sides are fixed and immovable. He jumbles heaven and earth together, the things most remote and opposite, who mixes these societies which are, in their origin, end, business and in everything, perfectly distinct, and infinitely different from each other."* But that distinction the Church was only too ready to accept.

But that failure must not blind us to the achievement of the Church at the Reformation in finding in the family a new pattern of Christian living to take the place of the old monastic pattern. It was not a blind attempt to get back to the picture of the life of the Church in the book of *The Acts*. It was the attempt to find, according to the teaching of the Bible, a form of Christian living adequate to new conditions of life. The family became the new school of the Lord's service. It gave to the individual, emerging into a new self-consciousness and yet with his religious thinking still affected by the individualistic approach of the Middle Ages, a place where he knew that he was at home and where he could learn the Christian values of living in fellowship. We have only to try to imagine what would have happened if the family had not so developed to sweeten social life, to realise how great is our debt to it and how truly it was a new pattern of Christian social living.

6. THE CONGREGATION

ARE we to-day living still in the age of the Reformation? Sometimes when we look at the Church it would appear as if the Church thought so. A good deal of our theological thinking seems to imply that the

* Quoted in *The Orb and the Crown* by A. Vidler, p. 20*n*.

pattern of the Reformation can still be applied to our situation: that nothing has happened to ourselves and to the world to make a revaluation of that pattern as necessary as was a revaluation of the mediaeval pattern. " That this almost unimaginable change in man's outlook upon the universe and in his experience of day to day living must in course of time modify the expression of Christian theology and liturgy alike is self-evident, or at least one would have thought so were not theologians and liturgiologists apparently insensitive to and unaware of those changes to the subject matter of their studies and to the forms in which ultimate truth may be expressed."* And in our sociological thinking we seem in the Church even more clearly to accept the social pattern of the Church of the Reformation. When we speak of the Christian family we still tend to speak in terms of the Reformation family. We speak of preserving it as if its economic basis were not gone. We still seem to think that we can return to that rural economy of family and parish. It is time that we realised that for us the time of the Reformation is the Middle Age: mid-way, in development if not in years, between the Gospel age and the modern world.

Mr. G. M. Trevelyan tells us that " man has changed more in the last hundred years than in the previous thousand."† That means that Queen Victoria would feel more at home in the court of Alfred or Macbeth than we would in the first decade of her reign. We have to realise that something has happened—through the development of mechanical power, through the change from a rural to an urban society, through the concentration of power in new hands, through the growth of cities and the collection of men and women in large factories, through the end of the family as the basic economic unit and through the spread of education—to make our world an

* *Church Strategy in a Changing World* by Leslie Hunter, p. 12.
† *English Social History* by G. M. Trevelyan, p. 97.

entirely different place from what it was in the beginning of last century and to make the old pattern of Church life quite inadequate. But is the world typified by these changes the world in which we now live?

Or is that age of the Industrial Revolution already past for us? Has the age of Capitalism, based on expanding markets and on competition, already gone? Has the pace of development so accelerated that the one tragic error we can make is to think that the twentieth century is a continuation of the nineteenth? Or is it true, as Professor John MacMurray says: " We are living through the first world revolution. . . . For its goal is the unification of the world in a common life "* ?

Nothing is more urgent for the Church than that it should read the signs of the times and know the conditions under which it is living. The genius of Basil and Benedict and of the Reformers was that they knew that they were living in a critical age and that only revolutionary plans for the Church were possible. Devotion and piety may run into the sand if they take no account of the needs of men. Certainly the missionary work of the Church is utterly dependent on an acute reading of history. In a world in which half the world rejoices in the fact of revolution, for the Church to deny that it is living in a time of change at all is to condemn itself to the cloister. There is only one thing more important for Christians than this necessity of recognising this revolution in our life and that is the readiness to live their lives in the light of the glory of the Lord. That is the prime task and it is perhaps only as we do so that we can read the signs of the times.

If we are to see our situation to-day and hear the call of God to His Church we need particularly to appreciate what happened to the pattern of Church life during the Industrial Age—the age before our own. It is always

* *Conditions of Freedom* by John MacMurray, p. 35.

most difficult to assess the period before our own: to be critical of the things we take for granted and to be just to the things against which we rebel. We have to recognise all that we owe to the Church of our immediate fathers. We have to appreciate their problems and their achievements. We have to see what they did and what they failed to do before we can fully understand what we are called upon to do. In our inevitable tendency to regard the Victorian age as one of security and complacency and easy confidence we are all too apt to forget that the last hundred and fifty years was a time of great activity and expansion in the Church. By the end of the nineteenth century the pattern of Church life in this country had changed almost out of recognition from the pattern prevalent in the eighteenth century which had been set by the Reformation. And its significant expression was in the life of the congregation.

The evangelical revival, which owed its origin to Wesley, and, to a lesser extent, the Oxford Movement and the Disruption were part of a revolution in the Church in its attempt to adjust its life to the changing conditions in the economic life of the country. It was to the new classes made conscious of their position by the development of industry that Methodism appealed: to men in despair, to men condemned to a strange new life, to men raised to unaccustomed wealth and power. It was these men that Methodism followed into the new factory towns of Lancashire and elsewhere. Behind the more ecclesiastical controversy of the Disruption was the sense of the new social needs of men in the towns and cities of Scotland. And in the Oxford Movement, for all its detachment from immediate economic issues and its seeming passion for the past, was the conviction of the need of the Church to live its own life if the Church was to be free to win men.

Through these movements and in all Churches there was developing a great increase in the width of congregational activity and of depth in the Christian life of individual members. This growth of social religion and of personal piety was not confined to any section of the Church and was the great mark of the age.

We see the setting of this best perhaps in the birth and growth of societies of all kinds outside the official organisation of the Church. In these societies—philanthropic, missionary and educational—Church people took a leading part and their motive was always avowedly Christian. Their rise was something quite new in the history of the country and of the Church. They represented the new power and impetus of the prosperous Middle Class. They were quite different from the Christian political group—the Levellers, the Diggers, and others—of the seventeenth century. These movements were in our history the only attempts to apply Christian teaching in a radical way to our social and political life. They failed and have had no successors. Their members were struggling to get something for themselves and for other men: to get the chance of living a fully Christian life as they saw it. The great societies founded in the nineteenth century were not struggling to get anything but to give: to give to others what they were quite sure they had themselves. Their motive was philanthropy. They could afford to be philanthropic because their supporters had economic and political power. They were able to be philanthropic because they had a passion based on personal piety.

But it is only the rich who can be philanthropic in that kind of way. And the Church was rich. How wealthy many men were and how Christian the middle class we often forget. Such men were aware of their power, their privilege and their worth. They were moved by a mixture of horror, compassion and fear when they regarded the ignorant masses of the new towns. They believed in themselves as individuals and accepted their duties and

responsibilities as they saw them. "The real strength and felicity of the Victorian Age lay . . . in the self-discipline and self-reliance of the individual Englishman, derived indeed from many sources, but to a large extent sprung from Puritan traditions to which the Wesleyan and Evangelical movements had given another lease of life."*
But they believed also in the iron laws of economics. They accepted the division so clearly marked by Locke. Such a man as Shaftesbury, so passionate in his pity for the suffering poor, believed that nothing could be done by economic means to change their lot. Indeed their passion and their charity were in conflict with their economic theories and this is perhaps the reason why their passion was so intense.

The internal life of the congregations became the microcosm of this nation-wide philanthropy. Service to the less fortunate and cultivation of individual piety became the marks of Church life and led to the inauguration of social activities within a congregation. Sunday Schools, Bible Classes, Men's Meetings, Mothers' Meetings, Savings Banks, Temperance Societies, cultural and athletic societies all came into existence at this time and set a new pattern of congregational life. The vitality of this movement was remarkable and on its memory we still live. It was a vigorous Church life which met the needs of the class which set the pace and thinking of the Church, the rapidly expanding Middle Class. "The Victorians did respond to the needs of their day, they did make the patterns of Church life appropriate to their times."†

We see this vitality in the great expansion of the Church and we see, too, its basis in the direction of that expansion. The Church followed the people into the new terraces and villas that were being built on the outskirts of the

---

* *English Social History* by G. M. Trevelyan, p. 509.
† *The Christian Laity* by Kathleen Bliss in *The Frontier*, April, 1950, p. 158.

cities. It was then that great new churches were built by all denominations with a wealth of expenditure unknown for centuries. They did it quite naturally and certainly without any hypocrisy because the people who lived there were the Church. The work of the Church on behalf of those who remained ' down-town ' was philanthropy.

And with this great intensification of the life of the congregation there went on at the same time the organisation of the churches, of all denominations, on a national scale. They organised their national societies. They opened their central offices. They became in themselves great national societies for the welfare of their fellow men. And so was built up that pattern of the Church's life which we now take so much for granted. But it was new in its activity and in its form.

It was with these social and philanthropic activities that the lives of most Christians were concerned. And the theological interest of the Church was most concerned with the questions which these activities raised. Controversy did not hinge on national questions nor on strictly theological questions but on the liberty of the Church to live its own life within its borders according to its own conscience. It is this passion that links together the Oxford Movement and the Disruption in more than date.

The mind and passion of the Church were thus set on its own liberty and well-being at home and on its task of preaching the Gospel abroad. The interest of the Church was focussed either very much at home—on the Christian life inside the Church—or very much abroad—on the evangelization of the world. And, except for philanthropy, the middle distance of neighbourliness was not the Church's concern. The Christian Socialists were so unique and so outside the ordinary life of the Church that inside the Church they aroused little comment and even a faintly amused interest among those who felt that they belonged to another world. Their message and their actions influenced the direction of philanthropy but mainly outside the ordinary life of the Church of England, and two generations had to pass before the thinking and the life of the Church of England were in any way radically affected.

This vital congregational life was based on the Reformation conception of the family and on unquestioning acceptance of the economic order. What Wesley and his successors of all denominations did was to make the Christian domestic virtues which belonged to a rural economy rule in the homes of those who belonged to a new world of industry and commerce. They brought a new moral rectitude based on individual responsibility into the new towns and villages among the members of the new middle classes. What we call the hypocrisy of the Victorian age is only the index of the success of their teaching. But it was a rectitude which did not seriously question the economic basis of society. It was content to condemn popular protest and to equate poverty with sin.

In general M. Elie Halevy's caustic words about Methodism are applicable to the Church as a whole: " The evangelism of Wesley and Whitfield, in many respects remorselessly fanatical, had learnt to adapt itself to the economic requirements of North-West England and displayed the greatest indulgence towards all the business methods of the speculative financier and promoter. Here also a fusion took place between two opposed tendencies. There came into existence a class of austere men, hard workers and greedy of gain, who considered it their two-fold duty to make a fortune in business and to preach Christ crucified. This class had its hypocrites but it had also its saints—zealous philanthropists, who were, however, possessed of the practical turn of mind which enabled them to effect their schemes of benevolence without self-impoverishment."*

* *The History of the English People* by E. Halevy, Vol. II, p. 114.

Christian ethics was concerned primarily with how a man spent his money, not with how he made it. For it is in his home and from his home that a man spends his money and it was with his home and not with his place of work that the Church had to do. Christian stewardship—the responsible use by the individual of his money—was the Christian virtue. And the Church was essentially the Church of those who had something to steward. That is not to say that there were not many poor people in the Church. But the thinking of the Church was the thinking of a wealthy society. The lay leaders of the Church were chosen as much for their wealth as for their piety. This is certainly not to suggest that there were not many rich men who used their money most conscientiously and most unselfishly and were most scrupulous in how they made it.

Thus the great achievement of the Church in the last century lay in this growth of the life of the congregation, in the inculcation of the ideals of individual rectitude and philanthropic service in the middle class and in the new evangelistic enterprise of the Church abroad. But there is another side to the picture, as there was another side to the nation. The Industrial Revolution had led to so rapid and extensive a rise to power of the manufacturer and the merchant that they could be said to constitute a new class in society. The strength of the Church was that it could adapt its life to suit them and to influence them, both those who had attained great wealth and power and those who were only in a small way. But the Industrial Revolution brought another class into existence—the city proletariat. The destitute were, indeed, no new fact in Scotland. At the end of the seventeenth century Andrew Fletcher of Saltoun had estimated that one-fifth of the population of Scotland was destitute: that out of a population of one million " there were no fewer than two

hundred thousand people begging from door to door."*
He advocated slavery as the only means of dealing with
them. Disease, in the main, saved him the trouble. But
this was a different, a new problem. These were men who
were wanted. These were the men on whom the new
prosperity of the cities depended. Without their labour
the factories would be idle. Disease still did its best.
From 1825 to 1835 the death rate in Glasgow rose from
1 in 41 to 1 in 31. In 1847 it was 1 in 19. Typhus and
cholera were common. In 1854 one-third of deaths of those
over five years old were due to phthisis. In the first ten
days of that year there were 234 deaths from cholera.†
Disease came to be seen as an obstacle to efficiency, but
not till it invaded the upper classes.

The Church was not indifferent to this new, miserable
and teeming population of the towns. It still in the main
equated poverty and sin. It did not believe that anything
could be done to change the basic conditions of living and
employment. It could still declare that such suffering
was the act of God. Indeed some parish ministers in
Scotland declared that the potato famine was God's
judgment on the Disruption. The Church was active in
philanthropic work and in preaching, and there were those
who saw that more was needed. " The common idea
at present is that the whole function of the Church is to
teach and preach the Gospel; while it is left to other
organisations, infidel ones they may be, to meet all the
other wants of our suffering people. And what is this
but virtually to say to them, The Church of Christ has
nothing to do as a society with your bodies, only with
your souls, and that, too, but in the way of teaching ?
Let infidels, then, give you better houses and better
clothing, and seek to gratify your tastes and improve your

* *Andrew Fletcher of Saltoun* by W. C. Mackenzie, p. 87.
† From tables in *A History of the Working Classes in Scotland* by Thomas Johnston, pp. 298-301.

THE CONGREGATION

social state:—with all this, and a thousand other needful things for us as men, we have nothing to do."* But the constant preaching of the Church and the practical efforts of a few of its members had little effect because the type of Church life offered to these men had little relation to the lives they were living.

What was this proletariat ? Where had they come from ? Were they " those ' lapsed classes ' which form in all large cities, the mighty problem of Christian philanthropy ? "† Or were they " the city proletariat, the people who have never left the Church for the reason that they have never been in it ? "‡ Which description is true ?

It is a surprise to most of us to learn that, according to a census of all church attendances taken on a typical Sunday in 1851, only 19% of the population of Glasgow went to Church.§ We have been brought up in the tradition that in Victorian Scotland everyone went to Church twice a Sunday. And that was probably true of the middle class in Scotland. But there was another section of the population who were never in Church. There is a vivid description of what Dr. Norman MacLeod saw in Glasgow in 1848 during a serious riot. " Suddenly the leading thoroughfares were swept by a torrent of men and women of a type utterly different from the ordinary poor. Haggard, abandoned, ferocious, they issued from the neglected haunts of misery and crime, drove the police into their headquarters and, for a while, took possession of the streets."¶ But behind this riot was more than the wildness of the depraved. It came at a time of fierce political agitation and followed a Chartist meeting in

---

*Dr. Norman MacLeod speaking in 1852—*Memoir of Norman MacLeod* by Donald MacLeod, pp. 228.

† *Memoir of Norman MacLeod* p. 226.

‡ Dr. Kathleen Bliss in *The Frontier*, April, 1950, p. 140.

§ *The Second City* by C. A. Oakley, p. 113. In 1881 it was 18.7%.

¶ *Memoir of Norman MacLeod*, p. 190.

the City Hall. But "there is no evidence that the rioting was anything else than a spontaneous outbreak of hungry and enraged men, still less that the Chartists had anything to do with its direction."*

It is the fact of this other Glasgow, this other Scotland, that is important. These people were certainly not in the Church. But from where had they come ? And who now are their descendants ? Some, of course, were Irish. " By 1850 about one-fourth of the population of the industrial areas was Irish."† And certainly their plight was the worst of all. But the great majority were Scotsmen: men and women driven out of the country places by clearances and poverty and drawn to the towns by the hope of a new life in industry. They came from a rural life in which the pattern of Christian family life still held. They came into a life in which that life could survive only when prosperity or grim determination held. For most the pattern of the old life must have broken very soon. The appalling slums, the long factory hours, the lack of their accustomed social contacts would quickly crush all ability to hold to the old pattern of life except in the most resolute. And then there was the shortness of life. In the slums infant mortality was high, but so was adult mortality. And a high adult mortality has greater social consequences. Generation succeeded generation much more quickly in the slums than in the west end. When parents die in early middle life, at latest, their children have little chance of acquiring their traditions of adult life. Familiar traditions soon die out. The place of the elderly in maintaining such traditions is very important. And when these family traditions belonged to a life they had left behind them, then traditions are not likely long to survive in unfamiliar conditions which contradict them. It was these people whose traditions had been destroyed by the

* *History of the Working Classes in Scotland*, p. 254.
† *Ibid*, p. 278.

conditions in which they had to live who formed the mass of the working people of Glasgow. They were outside the Church. Few of the third generation of immigrants had probably been inside a church. The Church expressed a life that was now quite unfamiliar to them. There were families—such as David Livingstone's at Blantyre—who held to the old life. And there were others. And these are the ones of which we know. There were others who, because of the strength of that tradition, became the leaders of the working class movement. And we know something of them. But the important ones for our purpose are those who left no record, who were absorbed in that teeming population outside the Church. For they were the great majority.

We often say that in recent years the working man of Scotland has given up the Church. It would be far more true to say that he had never been in it. What has happened is that with the growth of education and the improvement in housing and in the general conditions of life the old cruel distinction between the two Glasgows has outwardly been to a certain extent erased. There is much more contact between the two, in tram, at sport, and even at work. The two have a better chance of knowing what each is thinking. And that has revealed the difference. But who are the descendants of those who joined the bread riots in Glasgow a hundred years ago? It would be revealing to know how many of their descendants are now in the churches in the new housing areas and what proportion of the descendants of those who, from the terraces and villas went regularly to church each Sunday, are now quite outside the Church.

The Church with its clear ideas of family life based on a secure rural community and of the stewardship of property could, despite its oratory and its loving service, do little to incorporate those who had lost the pattern of their lives and could find no other. Their thinking, based on a life of insecurity and early death, with little individual privacy and a growing sense of solidarity in misery and rights, could not be assimilated to the thinking of the Church. Their needs were different. So were their virtues.

But the pattern of family life was also only an inherited tradition for the middle class. It survived only because there had been no break in family fortune, and because their members lived longer, and because the Church had found it not too difficult to adjust its life to their new needs. But the middle class family in the city did not for long maintain the old pattern. The greatly increased division between home and place of work and the education of women, bringing with it their entry into most spheres of work, have radically altered that old pattern of life. There is little resemblance now between the well-to-do family of father and mother and one or two children in their bungalow or flat, detached from their neighbours and with no sense of belonging to a community, and the family of seventeenth or eighteenth century Scotland.

The idea that the family is the basic unit of Christian social living has ceased to be true of the middle class, even as it was never true of the working class. And with that change the congregation has lost its roots in the common life of men.

But there is still a third factor which has to be taken into account when we try to see what was happening to the pattern of Church life during the last hundred and fifty years. The foreign missionary enterprise of the Church may seem to have little to do with what we have been describing. But it had an important place in the life of the Church and may well prove to have had a significant, if prophetic, influence on the future pattern of the Church's life.

That enterprise marked the recovery of a note that had become almost completely silent in the age of the Reformation. The Reformed Church of the seventeenth century was content to believe that God meant Moslems to be Moslems and Hindus Hindus and almost ridiculed any suggestion of preaching the Gospel to every creature. And with the refusal to believe that in Christ there was no distinction of race, the missionary task of the Church died. The recovery of that note is one of the mysteries of the Church and was probably due in the main to the evangelical revival with its emphasis on a passionate faith and on a vocation of witness.

It may be that the Church unconsciously turned to work abroad because it could do little at home because of its inability to enter the world of the proletariat. It may be that the Church found it easier to preach the Gospel to men who were in the primitive rural economy in which the Church itself had developed and to which its life was more easily adapted than to those living in the new conditions of industrial life. It is certain that the idea of the highest Christian vocation came to be interpreted in terms of missionary work abroad and that the conception of vocation as a call to serve God in the secular callings of ordinary life at home was lost.

Perhaps, in the providence of God, it was only by such a far-flung enterprise, only by bringing in the whole world and revealing to men's eyes that the Church was without distinction of race, that the Church could be enabled to see and to tackle the problem of evangelism in the new age, which will certainly prove to be not national but universal. Only, perhaps, when by the grace of God and the miracle of His working among men, the Church is seen as one, will the world itself be seen as one by the Church. The problem of finding the Christian pattern for a post-industrial age cannot be solved when treated nationally. The Church had to learn about itself abroad before it could see its task at home.

But it is a more practical side of the foreign missionary

enterprise that concerns us here. The earlier great work of missionary expansion was achieved largely through the instrumentality of the monastic communities. What was the instrument by which the modern missionary expansion was achieved ? That is a question that surely deserves some study. The Church cannot, for more than a hundred years have been sending out tens of thousands of men and women to an enterprise which has resulted, under God, in the visible fact of the world Church without having learnt something.

It is difficult at first to see any pattern at all. The missionary movement has been carried on in diverse and often make-shift ways. There has been nothing like the uniformity of the monastic pattern of life and work. There have, of course, been the monastic missionary orders. But these have not been typical. The pioneer period was peculiarly individualistic, as was, doubtless, also the work of the pioneer missionary monks in Northern Europe in the early centuries. The form of missionary life has rather been something that has grown up through the necessity of finding a way of working adapted to the task and the environment and was not one imposed by the Church at home. Men and women brought up and trained in the life of the Church at home have found themselves living as a community engaged in a common task in a land of an utterly different tradition. What has been the pattern of their life and work ? Again, superficially, we might say that there was no pattern: that they simply lived as they might have lived in a rather isolated society at home. But that is not so. The Christian family has had a large influence in missionary work abroad, but in no sense can it be said to have been the agent of mission. The congregation, as known at home, has not proved a thing that could be transported. And it certainly has not influenced the corporate life of missionaries. The overmastering difference has been that what united them has been the total job of evangelism which has swept away all of the divisions between family and work so familiar in congregational life at home. Because of the necessity of the work those sent out have had to find new ways of co-operation and a new pattern of Christian social living.

There are some factors in this that may seem obvious and even trivial but which are very important. The first is that almost from the first the missionary enterprise has included women as well as men. In fact for long the foreign mission field was the only place in the Reformed Church where women could fully use their gifts in directly Christian work. The second is that the missionary movement, like the early monastic movement, though not predominantly lay, yet included lay men and women as equal workers in their own professional callings. Missionary work is perhaps the only sphere of the Church's work where doctors, teachers, nurses, agriculturists and ministers bring their professional skills into a common service and work together in an equal comradeship. The third is that there has always been some form of economic equality among missionaries. The system of economic competition which operates at home and in the Church at home has never operated among missionaries abroad. The fourth is that this fellowship in work has always at least aimed at the inclusion of men and women of another race.

No one would pretend that you find on the mission field a perfect co-operation and a peace unknown at home. Each of the above four points, except the third, has caused endless discussion. But it has been discussion about real issues with which all were concerned. Doubtless the growing pains of the monastic movement in its first three hundred years were even more acute. But something was learned and achieved of real importance to the Church at home.

The peculiar significance of this world-wide experiment in co-operation on the mission field is that it touched the four points on which the Church at home had failed and which are the points on which the future of any new social life in our country now turns. The Church, since the Reformation, has refused to give to women a full place in its service: the world to-day gives women an almost equal place with men. The Church has not found how to bring the work of men in their daily vocations into the service of the Church: the world to-day recognises the need of a new co-operation in work. The Church has failed even to see the shame of her departure from the teaching of Jesus and the life of the early Church and has even adopted into its own ministry the economic competition of the world: the world to-day knows a new desire for, and sees the possibility of, economic justice. The Church has allowed itself to become, to a great extent, divided into race and nation: the world is certainly lost, and knows it, if it cannot find the way to racial co-operation. If the Church fails on those four points, it will fail to express the love of God in terms of man's greatest needs. And the missionary enterprise at least showed the foretaste of a pattern for the life of the Church in which these four needs are somewhat met. For, whatever be the form of the life of the Church in the future, it will survive as an effective missionary force only if that new pattern of life gives women their own place in it, and if it finds an integral and significant place for the work of laymen in their professions and crafts, and if it evolves a new economic life for itself nearer to the teaching of Jesus, and if it knows, not in theory but in glad experience, that it is a community open to all men, of every nation and race.

III
THE TASK TO-DAY

1. THE CHANGING PATTERN IN THE PAST.

WE have seen how the pattern of the Church's life has changed constantly down the centuries. Indeed the pattern has never remained the same for long. The common fabric of men's living has not itself remained constant. Their means of gaining food and their ways of living in families and social groups have changed with the development of their control over the forces of nature and with their contact with their neighbours. Since the first days of the Church the witness of Christian men to their faith has found itself called upon in each age to discover new forms of Christian living in which the love of God might be expressed. There has been that constant and unrecorded pattern, of which Professor Butterfield speaks,* of worship and preaching which in varying forms has kept men aware of their faith and without which there could have been no life. There has also been the persistent urge to translate that heard message of Salvation into a life in which that love is known as real. Without that response there never would have been a Church. That response has been there in all ages, directing and upholding men and women in faith and love. But in certain ages there comes a more urgent sense of the need of some new and more corporate and creative expression of that faith in the lives of men. It is of these critical ages that we have been thinking. Our sketch has been brief and fragmentary, dealing cursorily with the main epochs and then only in the most general of

* *Christianity and History* by Herbert Butterfield, p. 131.

terms. It has said nothing about the pattern of Church life, quite different from ours, of the Eastern Orthodox Churches nor of the new forms of Church life to be found to-day in the Churches of Asia and Africa. The whole subject of the economic forms of the Church's life in all its traditions and in all ages still awaits the study of some scholar. Our smaller concern has been only to catch a glimpse of the main points on the line of the development of our Church's life and our aim is the practical one of trying to see what kind of life our present situation demands. So we began with the beginning of the Church, with that small World-Church with which we must always begin if we are to know that our history begins in Christ Himself. We went on to follow the development of the Church in the West after the division of the ancient world, for that is the branch of the Church's history to which we belong. With the Reformation our concern was further narrowed to the record of our own Reformed tradition. And it ended with the more particular problem of the Industrial Revolution in our own land. This is not to suggest that this is the only, or the most important, line of Church history. It may well be that in the future the line of the Church's development may be seen to lead, not to us in the Reformed Churches of the West, but to the Church in China or in America. And it is certain that for the future development of a fully Christian life we shall need to be concerned not only with our own particular tradition but also with the traditions and discoveries of other Christians in other lands. But the line we have sketched is the line of our development. For us to-day, in our particular situation, it is imperative that we should understand the way in which our tradition has developed. Such a knowledge is a necessary condition if we are to try to answer the question which is being forced on us by events: What kind of life should we as Christians be trying to live in the world to-day?

CREATIVE SOCIAL LIVING—THE AGENT OF MISSION

One thing clearly emerges from our survey. The missionary task of the Church—its ability to extend the Gospel into new areas of life—has in the past depended on the creation within the Church of new forms of social living. The only instruments of evangelism are men and it is only as men have found the means of living together a creative social life that the Faith has spread. The lonely pioneer work of the missionary at the beginning of every age of expansion has often obscured this from us. We have forgotten that it is only when men have known a form of community in which their attempt to live the Christian life was free, or felt free, that they have been able to go out alone to preach the Gospel. You must have a Christian community before you can have a missionary. And wherever that missionary's work takes root you find growing up around him a new community. The Faith does not exist without this social expression.

These new creative societies have been of various forms and have arisen in many ways. Sometimes, as in the foundation of the monasteries, it has been the chaos of the world that has impelled men to form new cells of Christian living in the knowledge that only so could Christian life be lived at all. At other times, as at the Reformation, the emergence of economic and social groups has forced Christians to find a pattern of Christian life in terms of those groups. Again, at other times, as for instance in the modern missionary movement, there has been no conscious sense of a need to create something new but rather, in the demands of new tasks and in the experience of new conditions of life, a new pattern of life has almost unawaredly been shaped. What is certain is that new patterns of Christian social living have arisen to meet new challenges to the Faith and new opportunities of obedience, whenever there have been in the Church some who have heard the disturbing call of Christ. Doubtless there have been many missed opportunities and the response has at all times been but inadequate. But on that response the unchanging missionary task of the Church has depended.

OF LIFE, NOT OF ORGANISATION

Another thing that is clear is that it has not been the official action of the Church that has led to the formation of new patterns of life. No General Assembly, any more than any Pope or Council of the Church, has ever decreed a new pattern of Christian living, however much they may have felt the need and however warmly they may, at times, have welcomed attempts to meet it. It is not in the nature of institutions, whether ecclesiastical or political, to originate or propagate life. Such movements of life originate from the working of the Spirit among men personally. New political patterns come from the passions of men who are conscious of the possibility of better things for themselves and their fellows and who are willing to suffer to achieve them. And it is the power of their conviction and the truth of their experience which become, if they succeed, impressed upon institutions and so are made available for other men in later generations. Even more clearly, the life of Faith is alive in the daily living and thinking of men and women, if it is alive at all. And when, through hope or suffering, that life becomes on fire it may impress itself on the organisation of the Church, to be interpreted to other men. And so, as we have seen, new forms of Christian living arose through the experience, first, of individual men and, then, through that of groups of men who saw a new need and heard a new call. It is only as somehow that need has been strongly felt by other men and that call has answered their hopes that the new pattern of life has appeared intelligible to them and something creative and effective has happened in the Church.

So these new movements have arisen out of the consciousness of the needs of men in ordinary human life and out of the conviction that the life of Christ must be expressed in terms of common life. That is why these movements have, in origin, been lay rather than clerical—or rather they belong to that deeper stratum of life and faith where the distinction between lay and clerical disappears. They have belonged to the life rather than the organisation of the Church. And they have always arisen untidily and appeared as problems to the organisation of the Church. They have always, in some form, voiced the protest that the Church is not simply an ecclesiastical organisation but Christ's community of men and women. They have always recalled the Church to the original conviction that the Church is made up of men in their ordinary daily lives, redeemed and restored in Him Who claimed for Himself no other public title than the Son of Man and Who accepted a religious title only on the Cross. So these new movements, however diverse their form, have always sought to get back, in the words of the Scots Confession, to that 'which Christ Jesus himself did and commanded to be done.' Their strength has been in the desire of men to find a way of life nearer for them in their days to Jesus' teaching in order that they may do His work and express His love. They form, not strange episodes breaking the continuity of the Church's witness, but the very milestones and turning points of the Church's history.

Such experiments have never been made with cold calculation. Men have made them because they knew that this was the one thing that God had commanded them to do and they could do no other. But such obedience has never been blind. Men have heard the call because they knew the dangers that threatened men. They knew the impossibility of living in the old familiar setting as full a Christian life as they knew to be their duty. Benedict and Francis and the Reformers knew that the old pattern of Christian living was inadequate to their time; at least for them. They knew that the old was doomed but far more clearly they knew the light of Christ, even in the dreariness of their present lives. They were not fleeing from doom. They were seeking the life that they knew existed for them. It was joy that led them on. It was the certainty of that joy that made Benedict found his new society and Francis embrace poverty and the Reformers proclaim the rule of Christ. They knew that they must recover in their own lives the simplicity of Christ. They knew that the one thing needed in their day was 'a school of the Lord's service.'

They saw two things with such startling clarity that they knew that they had to obey whatever the cost to themselves. They saw the situation they were in and they saw Christ.

2. THE SITUATION WE ARE IN

IT is easy for us to look back on recent history and to see examples in others of the Church's failure to see the situation that Christians were in and to see Christ. We may think of the Church in Germany in the 'thirties. Shortly after Hitler's rise to power a German minister travelling in the Far East spoke to a gathering of missionaries in Moukden and shocked them by his entire indifference to the persecution of the Jews. On two points only did he express any uneasiness: one was the possible danger of the new regime to the Church as an institution, the other was abstract theological objection to the Nazi views on race. He unquestioningly accepted the idea that you can preach the will of God and yet be quite unconcerned with the sufferings of men. We see that failure clearly in others. Do we see it as clearly in ourselves? For instance are Christians in our country to-day deeply concerned with the situation which confronts us in Africa in our choice between a colonial policy which aims at the development of a Christian Africa and a policy based on racial discrimination? Is the Church as fully concerned as the Colonial Service is? In this situation of comparable racial danger do we see the situation and do we see Christ any more clearly than the German Church did? The question for us may well be as crucial.

There have, perhaps, been times when Christians did not need to do either in any self-conscious way. There may have been times when the situation seemed quite stable and Christ had no new demands to make. Perhaps the early middle ages were such a time. But assuredly ours is not such a time.

NO RETURN TO THE PAST

We blind ourselves to the facts and close our minds to any belief that this is God's world and His hands are at work in it if, from fear or false humility, we think that the world is much as it has always been. We have to acknowledge that we live in a world which is quite new to us: that the assumptions that we unconsciously make belong to a world that is already past.

Recently at a Conference a speaker in exposing the dangers of the Welfare State used numerous instances to constrast personal charity and the official charity of the community. But strangely typical were his examples. His instances of official charity were all in terms of large cities and of urban life. His instances of personal charity were all against the background of the village and the squire's daughter. He failed to deal with the fact that the large city had come into existence long before the Welfare State and there was no way by which the squire's lady could operate in the city, Welfare State or no Welfare State. Too often as Christians we fail to ask the question: "How in the city of Glasgow, with its streets and tenements and dislocated family life, are we going to express

Christian concern for persons?" but say to ourselves: "We prefer a simple pattern of life"—a simple pattern which has ceased to exist in Glasgow for at least one hundred and fifty years. There is no point in the Church or in individual Christians saying that the Love of God in Christ is more easily expressed within a small, interdependent, rural community if we are in fact called upon to live in the streets and tenements of Glasgow. To emphasise too much our preference for a more primitive social life is only to suggest that God's love is straitened, that it cannot save. For the sense of the individual's contribution, the type of independence and the privacy known to rural village life are no longer available to the working people of Glasgow, and God must be as much the God of Glasgow as of the country places.

The essence of a crisis is that we do not know what will happen and cannot turn back for guidance to any event in the past. In that sense our times are truly critical. Accustomed paths will lead us nowhere. Loyalty can no longer be an obedient clinging to abstractions that we have been taught to honour or a selfish defence of interests that we know are threatened. In a time of crisis loyalty can be only to people. For instance, if in our Welfare State the Church need perhaps no longer fear judgment for the material needs of Lazarus as he lies at its gate, the Church must still be loyal to Christ's love in concern for the spiritual insecurity of those outside and must know that that love can be met only by a full understanding of their real situation.

The world has changed before our eyes. We cannot go back to any pattern of the past.

NO RETURN TO CHRISTENDOM—GEOGRAPHICALLY OR ECONOMICALLY

There can, for us, be no possibility of a return to Christendom. There can never again be a compact little

Christian area of the globe, cut off from the rest of the world, knowing nothing of the great civilizations of China except the strange tales that Marco Polo brought back and which no one believed: cut off, too, from the utterly unknown worlds of Central Africa and America, and with the barriers up against the Moslem world, but, fortunately, not impregnable to its science and philosophy.

Such a compact world is gone for ever and we forget how long its tradition has lingered on in our imaginations to give the background of our thinking even when we talk in other terms, even when it is Christian men whose minds have opened new areas of thought and knowledge to the whole world. It is the tragedy of modern man's dismay and fear that the Church has seemed almost to cut off theology from his knowledge of the universe. Anthony West has said that the tragedy of modern man is that three hundred years ago the Church decided to know no more and since then man has been lost in the world. Even the most recluse of Christians is affected by this disintegrated knowledge of the universe and of man. If this only presses him into a more exclusive attachment to his (theological) world it does not deliver him from disintegration for he cannot escape from the world of other men's knowledge and testimony. It is of this confrontation of other men and their thinking we have to take account rather than of the one particular example of that thinking in Communism. The world now has no furthest limit: we can go only round and round.

NO RETURN TO NINETEENTH CENTURY EXPANSION—
ECONOMICALLY

There is, for us, no possibility either of return to that world of new territorial discoveries and of expanding trade which made international competition abroad and competitive capitalism at home seem the economic order of an unending hopefulness. That world of our grandfathers still seems to most of us the only comfortable world and our rightful due. We even dream of its return. But that world belongs to the past as truly as the idea of Christendom. There is now only the one world: the world of all men, the world now dependent on all its parts for its life. And it is God who has called us into that world. We have known that to be true in theory for long. We have confessed its truth in our prayers and in our praise. We know it now in our minds, if not yet in our bones. We know that we are affected in our lives and not only in our dividends by what happens to the peasants of China or to the miners of Africa. The problem is that we do not know what to do with the overwhelming problem of its reality. Our pain is that we know and yet cannot answer our knowledge with any creative thinking or with any action that seems capable of expressing our unity with other men.

OR PATERNALISTICALLY

The nineteenth century's picture of the relationship of what had been Christendom to the rest of the world was paternalistic. Not only on the religious side did men see themselves offering enlightenment in place of fear and health in place of disease, but in the secular world, too, men saw a future in which they expected that through the gradual expansion of the liberal tradition of Europe through education, trade contacts and imperialistic paternalism, Asia, Africa and all parts of the world would develop a liberal parliamentarianism similar to our own. Because there was reality in the gifts which we brought and because 'trade followed the flag,' very real developments took place. But now that day is over, although we see the fruits of that day.

Now we are confronted not so much with a world divided into two camps which seek different things as with a world all of whose societies seek the things that make for war and most of whose members desire the things that make for peace. It is self-interest that governs our actions in societies. It is mutual dependence that makes us into communities. And the interests of our societies have gained the upper hand, because their interests are clear and obvious and are hallowed now by old ways of thinking. Our sense of community finds only intermittent expression and an outlet only in dreams. Our community feeling is weak because it is expressed only in relationships that are private. We find it in strength only when a common danger threatens us. It is endlessly frustrated because world community has no reality.

OURSELVES IN THE SITUATION

So we cannot say that West is divided against East and that our danger is that we allow the values of the East to possess us of the West. We have now no right to say that callousness and cruelty, greed and covetousness are the prerogatives of Communist thinking and that we have allowed them to affect us. It is rather that we have let the natural ambitions of our societies, uncontrolled by any sense of community, have undisputed rule over us. Our protest against the things we have to do or the things done in our name becomes half-hearted. We become like Joseph of Arimathea who loved Jesus but could not see how He could rule in Jerusalem and so could offer Him only an honoured burial. It is our glad acceptance of God's rule in this world and of the way of His Son as our way in this world that makes us Christians.

To see our situation is not primarily to see the world but to see ourselves. Our task is not to look at the world as if it were something that exists outside ourselves and to try to see and understand and oppose what other men are doing in the world: though that exercise of seeing and understanding other men has its use for us, for one of the most necessary and most painful things we have to do is to lose the Victorian idea that we in Britain have a right to rule the world. Our task is rather to try to see and understand what we ourselves are doing, to recognise what is happening to ourselves. We're citizens of the world, thrown by history into the situation which our Faith has always professed to be the real situation and yet living our lives under a more open domination of selfishness, greed and callousness than we have ever known. We who have professed that all men are our brothers are forced for the first time to live with all our brothers. More fully than ever before we are called to Christian obedience, not in our worship only but in our life. We are faced with an outward situation which is indeed as critical as that which faced Augustine or Benedict or Francis or the Reformers. And it is a situation from which we can escape far less than they could.

THE AGE OF PRIVATE LIFE IS OVER

And it is not only that we are thrown into a new world situation. We cannot merely make the excuse that the setting is too vast for our small minds. For what is true of our bewildered citizenship of the world is true also of our private lives. It is not that we who are at home and actively Christian in our private lives suddenly find ourselves public citizens of the world and at a loss. If that were so then we might learn to translate our private loyalties into public duties and to make our affection for our friends grow into a wider compassion. We might resolve to treat all men as we treat our own. But we cannot, for our basic frustration is in our private lives. We do not know how to treat our own. We have talked about our right to live our own lives and we find that we are living them and that they are not what we want. For the revolution that has made us world citizens has altered the whole pattern of our private lives. It has at last revealed that the whole idea of having private lives is now a delusion, for what we call our private lives is built up on a very public use of other people's lives. The blasphemy of individualism has been exposed by the revelation of our dependence on others and of the necessity of our finding in some way community with them. It has also destroyed the illusion of smallness in which we could pretend to live for ourselves.

Our homes have ceased to be the natural basic unit of society. They are now only what we deliberately make them. They are no longer held together as units in the economic fabric of social life and so where there is no deliberate intention they disintegrate. Speaking of the years before the first world war, Sir Osbert Sitwell says: "The Age of Private Life, founded on the family, was nearing its end."* The private life of which he speaks may seem far removed from the more pedestrian lives of men even at that time. But just as the great houses of England were doomed to vanish before the onslaught of a new economic pattern, so middle class and working class lives were just as much becoming more individualistic and less integrated into a coherent pattern of community by reason of the changing economic and industrial pattern. The obligations and privileges of all members of British society were clearly defined and sustained by economic sanctions, but not only by economic sanctions, for so clear was the pattern that those who failed to fulfil their social obligations or transgressed the moral code of society were indeed outside the camp. This is what gives the point to innumerable novels and plays from Goldsmith's *Vicar of Wakefield* to Wilde's *Lady Windermere's Fan*. By contrast the modern man finds his social life not by fulfilling a code of social obligation on one level or another but in all kinds of self-chosen interests and activities and his transgressions are not against a code but against people and his exile or otherwise depends on their personal reaction. We are no longer part of a hierarchical society.

* *Great Morning* by Sir Osbert Sitwell, p. 231.

We now must choose our home life and make it what we will, even as we choose our work and our other social relationships. And so, for many, the relationships which daily work brings are as significant, or as meaningless, as their family relationships. For they, too, are what we make them and, of themselves, will do nothing. Our other social relationships—of sport, or Church, or social interest—are more consciously chosen and therefore seem to many the more vital. And so a new pattern of relationships has come into being, utterly different from the old given relationships of birth and community. And all bring their burden of personal choice and decision. And men feel weary and often frustrated. It's not a question of the old being better: at least that's not a question worth time arguing. It's a question of the new being different. We are individuals living of necessity in a changing society. We're trying, perhaps, to make that society a community. At least we feel it ought to be. We are, at least, making for ourselves citadels of familiarity where we may feel at home. For we cannot live as individuals. We must find relationship with others or make them. The one significant fact for us is that to-day we are more consciously individual than ever before. The other significant fact is that our necessary attempts to find community with others—in family, in work, in social groups, in Church—are all deliberate and must be so at our present stage.

It is a paradox of human nature that what, in our moments of insight, we know to be our need we still rebel against. Men have always rebelled and always will rebel against the demands of community, even though they acknowledge their dependence on other men. Therefore when our social relationships are chosen and escapable they are the more apt to be rocks of offence. The men and women of a village just as much as the dweller in the city tenement no doubt rebelled against and even repudiated their relationships of family and community but they could not escape them. The circumstances of their lives held them within these relationships. The tenement-dweller on the other hand fights to preserve his ties of family and community against his circumstances. It can, therefore, be seen how much more they are at the mercy of human rebellion and sin. Perhaps those of us who talk about the family and the sanctity of marriage should more often realise how much more these people are in need of support than of scolding. The trams in a Scots city on a Sunday evening, full of young parents with infants crossing the city from visits to their parents are evidence of the value these young people place on family ties but one has only to think for a moment to realise how imperilled are these ties. It is no wonder that many people find life exhausting and some find it frightening. It is an exhausting and a frightening thing to have to create the pattern of one's social life: it is much more comfortable to inherit it, geographically and economically provided. There are those who are finding through their creative actions a satisfying sense of community in their family, or, possibly, in their Church. But they are often blind to the fact that it is a new thing that they are finding and are blind, therefore, to the difficulties that face others. They often talk as if they were merely conserving the old family system or the old Church life. They don't realise that they are creating a new.

Our first task, then, is to see the situation we are in: and not merely to look at the world as if we stood outside it but to see ourselves in the world and to realise that it is a new world and that our call is to an obedience in new terms.

3. THE OTHER THING NEEDFUL

But we cannot do anything to find the way of building the life we know we must build unless at the same time we begin to see the other thing that the Apostles and Benedict, Francis and the Reformers saw. They saw not only the situation they were in: they saw Jesus.

Behind each new venture in Christian living was a vivid, an apocalyptic faith in Jesus which made life serious and hopeful. It was never simply the hope that the way of Jesus might bring good results. It was certainly never the despair of all else that suggested that His way might at least be tried. These men never said: " This is the only thing left that might save us." Theirs was an assured, joyful belief in the supreme importance of Christ. The only thing that mattered for them was their faith in Him. And that faith was not merely that He was their individual Saviour. It was faith in His relationship to their world. They declared that He was the Saviour because He was the Ruler of this world: that He would come in judgment and in glory. They had their apocalyptic vision of hope and fear. They declared to men the Last Things because in Christ they knew the end of the world. This is the part of their faith which we tend to pass over. It makes us uncomfortable. We study their activities with meticulous interest and gratefully assess their social and economic achievements and we disregard what was the mainspring of their faith and actions and dismiss it as superstition, or, at best, ignorance. Their insistence on the Coming of Christ, on His judgment and His glory makes us uncomfortable. We pretend that we have no need of such inducements to belief: that we will serve Christ with no thought of fear or of reward. But our reluctance is radical: it is a determined reluctance to take Jesus and His relationship to this world seriously. We do not really believe that God has created the world and has redeemed it in Christ. We see no purpose in our own lives and so we can see no purpose in Jesus's life except to comfort us in our escape from this world. We see no purpose in this world and so we refuse to see that the only conceivable end for a world made by God is in the power and judgment and glory of Christ.

It was because they took Jesus with absolute seriousness that the men of the early Church believed that He would come. What else could it mean to believe in the Creation, the Incarnation, the Resurrection? How else could their hope be expressed? So they not only prayed that He should come quickly: they believed that He would come. It was this belief in His rule, present and coming, that made them a household of faith, obedient to His way of life. Without this faith they would have been merely a society.

In the beginning of the Dark Ages the leaders of the monastic movement took heed of another world than the world of men's construction that was crumbling around them. That world of Christ's rule was the real world, because Christ was real. And in their faith in the supremacy and relevance of that world alone they set out to live a new kind of life to His glory.

With the Reformation men's vision of the nature of that other world changed. It had become remote from this world, a place of grim terror and of undecipherable joys, whose entrance men made one by one at death. Christ's Kingdom belonged to the shades. The compelling vision of the Reformers was of Christ's rule in the affairs of men now. Their belief was in the Sovereignty of the will of God now and of the crown rights of the Redeemer in this world. But theirs was no less an apocalyptic faith because it was so closely concerned with this world.

The modern Missionary Movement, in more hidden and devious ways, rediscovered the Lordship of Christ over all men. Because of this the Church was called to a new obedience and its members to a new apostleship. Their sustaining faith was not merely to try by men's endeavours to make Christ's rule extend over all the world but to declare to men that He did rule and that His rule was Love. Their prayer was that men's blindness and disobedience should not prevent the evangelization of the world in their generation. That, too, was an apocalyptic faith.

Was it all delusion? We can, indeed, see how in each age the expression of that faith was formed by the needs and the thinking of the time. We can say that each age had its own, its one-sided and perhaps its exaggerated, picture of what that faith meant. But that is not to say that that faith is not essential. It is not even to say that any of the single emphases was false. What seems the exaggeration is the hyperbole of love. Love of Christ and faith in Him made men use expressions that seem exaggerated, because men's words are weak and their understanding inadequate. But that love and that faith are not exaggerated. For it is only as men believe that Christ is King, not by the election of His citizens but in His own right, that they can obey Him with joy and hope and can gladly enter into new experiments of living for His glory. It is only as men believe that Jesus really matters that they will die for their faith. And equally it is only as they believe that He really matters that they will live by it. The creative acts of devotion and of love have always sprung from the conviction of men that to do the Christian thing is of supreme importance, and that Christ rules for them whatever be the outcome. That is true of the heroic, loving actions of simple Christian men and women in all ages. It is as true of those who have sought to create something new and living in their social life.

It is this assurance of Christ in the present that alone brings glory and joy now. For He is not a hope or an ideal whose realization depends solely on our efforts and whom events seem constantly to disprove. He is known now in His love. He is known now to hold the power of God. He is known now in His gifts to men in personal and practical ways. And this conviction of His presence and of His rule now is the spring of love and hope and life. It is this that links the saints with the artists in their assurance of the glory known to men in the earthly and in the strength that comes of knowing that what is done for the sake of that glory is of abiding significance. For Christ is seen, if He is seen at all, as beauty is seen of the artist, in the world of our reality: not in a minute analysis of cause and effect, nor in some of the facts, but in the impact of the whole on our awakened spirits. It is thus that man hears God speak. It is in that vision that man knows in his heart that Christ rules. When that apocalyptic vision fades the life of faith, so called, becomes a striving, and a grudging comment, and love dies.

There will be for us no meeting of our situation with creative hope unless somehow we see Jesus with the clarity with which they saw Him. Can we see Him ready to roll up this age as a worn garment and to usher in His new age on earth as did the early Church? Can we see Him as the Eternal Lord with arms outstretched in pity and in power, as on the dome of a Romanesque Church, and know that our own task is to sing His praise, as did men in the Dark Ages? Can we see Him as ruling this world in all its events and calling on His saints to rule with Him in their families and in their daily vocations, as did the Reformers? If these seem strange pictures to us, is it not because He has still to appear to our changed vision in some new picture of His rule; more socially, more universally, more personally, more intimately and still more gloriously? And if that vision is still to be given, is it not our duty to follow its leading in the ways, however hard, that are revealed to us? For certainly, if we have not that faith which believes without seeing, we shall never see Him.

4. THE EMERGING PATTERN

WE live in a time of catastrophic change. The only thing we know for certain is that the world will never be the same again. Our feeling of frustration and uncertainty is only the index of the changing conditions in which we live. It is never given to those who live through the crises of the world's history to see clearly what is happening. The men who heard tell of the fall of Rome, the men who knew the bewilderment of the Reformation, did not feel that they were living at a critical time of the world's history. It is only we, who look back and who have learned to think in terms of the measurement of time, who label epochs as critical or otherwise and in so doing have ourselves become self-conscious. These men knew only that things were not as they had been and did not look as if they would ever be so again. They knew that things were very difficult and that they did not know clearly what to do and yet that they must act. The change that we know now in our lives is certainly greater and more rapid than anything they experienced and it involves the whole world. No wonder we are dismayed and bewildered and uncertain. No wonder there is an almost inescapable temptation for Christians to think that all that is possible for them, or all that is required of them, is that they be faithful in the little things, in the things they know, each in his little corner. But that is not to see Christ as King. That is not to believe that this is God's world. That is certainly not what Jesus meant when He told His disciples that they must be faithful in the least, if they would be faithful in much.* We have to remember that He first told the parable of the Unjust Steward, as if we have first to learn the lessons of that parable before we could dare to undergo His tests of faithfulness. And what were these lessons ? That only the man who faces

* *Luke* 16, 10-12.

the catastrophe that threatens him and seeks with all the means at his disposal for the way of his salvation will ever do anything in the way of faithfulness: that in the end what matters is what binds us to other people, our entry into their lives. It was for that two-fold wisdom that the Unjust Steward was commended. Only when we begin to learn these lessons will we begin to be faithful and our faithfulness will then be tested in the use we make of material things and only at the end, when we have learned faithfulness there, will we get what is our own.

Jesus said: " If ye have not been faithful in that which is another man's, who shall give you that which is your own ? " Now faithfulness is an active virtue, having to do with the use we make of our time, of our money, and of our life. And in Christ's teaching that is clearly a matter of taking thought. He expects us to heed the signs of the times. He expects us to ask ourselves whether we are faithful stewards or asleep. We must ask ourselves: " What is the kind of life that Jesus calls us to live to-day ? What are the ways by which His love can be most real to us in our own lives and most recognisable as a light for other men ? What is the form of social living in which His Spirit can best be expressed to-day ? And what are the first steps which are already clearly revealed to us ? "

Therefore to refuse to give thought to the form of the Church's life is to fail in faithfulness. We have to ask ourselves what kind of life Christians ought to be living ? What are the things that they ought to be doing ? What are the dangers that threaten the Church's life ? And, above all, how should Christians be organising their life together ?

THE PATTERN FOR US CANNOT BE MONASTIC

It is certain that for us no return to a monastic pattern of life is possible. That was possible in an age of social and economic disintegration when the means of livelihood was individual and when all corporate organisation was weak and threatened. It was then possible and right for individuals to gather themselves together to create a new social life of Christian obedience for themselves. The problem for our age is not that of economic disintegration but of economic integration in one world for the first time in history. We cannot, even if we would, withdraw into economic self-sufficiency. This is not to say that there is no place in the world for the monastic life. There is. But the purely contemplative life is only possible now if it rests on the active life of a Christian community and, in fact, most monastic orders are now active in service. The monastic pattern is not likely to be the creative pattern for the life of the Church in a new age.

NOR CHRISTENDOM

Even less can we to-day attempt to rebuild a little Christendom. That achievement depended on clearly defined frontiers and a common acceptance of authority. The West may be the heir of Christendom and, indeed, owes the strength of its tradition to the fact of Christendom. But by no stretch of faith can we identify the West now with Christendom.

NOR THE OLD IDEA OF THE FAMILY

We cannot reconstruct the old idea of the Christian family as the basis of Christian social life, for we have destroyed its foundation. That idea of the family was based both on a family economy and an economic individualism, and both are gone. The family is indeed the primary unit of social life but it now exists, as it were, in a vacuum, awaiting all kinds of possibilities for its development. Not long ago, for example, a group of people set themselves to tabulate on one hand the tasks of the modern middle-class maidless housewife and on the other the social obligations of her grandmother as a young wife fifty years ago with two maids undertaking all the housework. When allowance had been made for time expended on receiving and returning calls, attendance at obligatory functions—at homes, dinner parties, calls—and the performance of duties of hospitality, they concluded that the modern young wife in the first year of her marriage, despite all the chores, had twice the leisure for company of her own choice and for amusements with her husband than was given to her grandmother. Now without doubt these social duties often seemed pointless and formal and were to young couples a severe trial to the flesh but they formed the framework of privilege and duty in a social community which supported the marriage relationship through stresses which often break it to-day. It is now free from the old bonds of authority. But it has not found its own pattern. When it becomes self-conscious it becomes isolated. The self-contained flat and the bungalow become citadels of isolation. The present tendency to the isolation of the family is a threat to any attempt to create community and a menace to the marriage relationship and therefore to the family life of the child. The family can find its own life only as it knows itself an integral part of a larger group. Just as political science knows that limits must be put to power, so knowledge of human frailty shows us the dangers of leaving the marriage or parental relationships unsupported or undisciplined by wider social ties. It is easy for us to see the sin and terror of Nazi or Communist undermining of fundamental human relationships. But it is dangerous for us not to be aware that, unless new vitality is given to the small social groupings in our own country, frenzied defence of our life against alien ideologies will only result in the strengthening of two forces which can be utterly destructive of community: the power of the state over the individual and the selfishness of the family. In Christian thinking a full community life is a necessity alike for a strong marriage relationship and a healthy national life.

NOR THE CONGREGATION AS WE KNOW IT

Last century saw the development of a new kind of social life in the congregation. But congregational life, as we have known it, is unable to meet the needs of the new situation, though it may be that out of congregational life the new pattern may emerge. But in its origin and development it has been too exclusively bound to the thinking of one class and too firmly detached from consideration of the political and economic sides of life for it to face the problem of a new age without reformation. The achievement of the Church of the nineteenth century was that it met the needs and moulded the ambitions of the middle class in its rise to power and its tenure of power. Its failure now is due to the fact that the position of that class has changed and the virtues it taught, of independence, temperance and philanthropy, are now inadequate. These virtues, as taught by the Victorian Church, depended on the privilege of possessions. When that privilege goes, these virtues lose their pre-eminence and demand a new interpretation. The Church is in danger of failing to see that the values it would defend are the values of the class to which its members belong and not the values of its Faith. And this danger is the greater because the Church in its congregational life has been concerned almost solely with the area of the private and leisure life of its members. Congregational activities have had as their aim the propagation of interest in, and the raising of money for, the work of the Church, the providing of a safe social life for its youth and the encouragement of a feeling of fellowship among its members, generally on a spiritual or a social level. And the teaching of the Church has been in terms of what its members should do in their homes and in their private relationships with other men. It has had little to do with what men did in their work. Not only has the Church had no interest in what its members do to earn their living: in many cases it does not know. ' To talk shop ' is as much out of place in a Church as it is in a mess. This pattern of congregational life has become so fixed that it affects what are called 'industrial' congregations as much as suburban. This convention, which was accepted and understood a hundred years ago, becomes an offence to men who are vitally concerned with the problem of the purpose of their work. It is one of the reasons why working men are reluctant to go to Church. They feel that the Church is not interested in them as men.

This is not to suggest that there is not in most congregations a true devotion and a real desire to be used by God for the salvation of men. That devotion and that desire are there but they are frustrated by the inability of Church-members to find the thing to do. They had their glimpse of new ways in the foreign missionary work into which they poured much of their enthusiasm. But that enterprise was too distant and too vicarious for any lessons to be learned at home. It showed, however, how men and women trained in the narrower interests and traditions of the Church at home could break through into a fuller social life when a new environment and new demands forced them to be free.

THE PATTERN MUST BE NEW

The new form in which the Christian life must be lived and the Faith expressed and which can alone be the instrument of God's purpose for the world cannot simply be any of the old patterns brought up to date. It must, of course, take something from each of the old patterns: the freedom of the individual to detach himself from old ways, which was the basis of monasticism; the conception of the family as the natural school for learning the co-operation of young and old, of men and women; the width and many-sidedness of the congregational group. But the new form must be neither of dependent individuals nor of independent families. It must express the interdependence of the age into which we have moved. Its economic form can be neither the absolute separateness of the monastery in which the individual gave up all he possessed and gained complete security nor the detached independence of the family. " Christian fellowship must begin to imply at least some mutual economic responsibility as inherent in its nature."* It must be in terms of the economic inter-dependence in which we now live. It must be a fellowship of families rather than of individuals and it must include our wider dependence on those with whom we live and work. The development of our social legislation gives us, indeed, the framework. We now know ourselves to be no longer merely private persons. But the framework has to be clothed in living tissue if it is to work. It is the duty of Christians to-day to make experiments in co-operative social living which will point the way to this new living society. In the Dark Ages when the framework of social life was collapsing, the Church through its monastic communities preserved the Faith and civilization. At the Reformation the Church made the family the bearer of a new life and gave the social setting to a new conception of the individual person. As the Church in those ages found the form of life not only for its own members but for all men within its range, so the Church to-day must find in its own life the pattern of life for men in this age.

The nature of that pattern will not be of our choosing but of God's ordering. The Church denies its faith in God's providence if it regards all that is happening in the world as man's apostasy or the devil's work and sees its task only as that of preserving isolated communities in the midst of an alien world. The nature of that pattern will be, of necessity, in terms of sharing and of inter-dependence. For that necessity is of God. We have to

* *We Shall Rebuild* by G. F. MacLeod, p. 131,

make our social inter-dependence and our public responsibilities the deliberate expression of our Faith, as, in the past, we have made our private duties. The Church, if it is to find its own life, has to find it in the pattern of the life of all men to-day.

For we can be quite sure that some new form of Christian corporate life will emerge in the world. To refuse to believe that is to refuse to believe in God. Already there are groups in other countries that are making the experiment. Already there are different patterns of Christian living to be found in the younger Churches of Asia and Africa. It may well be from these that the new world-pattern will emerge. Our problem is simply that of obedience—of doing the things that are revealed to us and of leaving events to mould the form.

And what are the things that are revealed to us? In other words, what are the definite ways in which quite clearly such pioneer groups must experiment? There are, at least, three.

5. THE THREE ESSENTIALS

SEEING ALL ITS MEMBERS FULLY AS PERSONS

THE first essential is that any Christian group which is seriously trying to find the way of Christian living for to-day must be concerned with all the personal relationships of its members. We have in the Church talked much about the sanctity of the individual. But, in fact, we have tended more and more to treat people as functions and to deal with only a section of their lives. Even the worship of the Church touches only a small part of the lives of the worshippers. We have already mentioned the Church's disregard of the working life of its members and that is the major portion of their life. To-day that part of men's life raises new problems of personal relationship: in a man's attitude to his fellow-workers, to his boss and to the purpose of his work. When all that is neglected, men are not being regarded as persons. An even greater question is the place of women. In nothing, as we have seen, has the Reformed Church been so uncreative as in its attitude to women. They have been treated not as persons, but as functions—as wives and mothers. The Church has forgotten that when God created man, He created man male and female. And, as has been wisely said, something goes wrong with any society which denies that. The Church can never find the new pattern until it abandons its opinion that God made man male only. And this may well be the greatest test. For it is not a matter of finding a new functional place for women in the Church, or even an equality in terms of men. It is not a question of women doing or not doing the work of men. It is a question of women being allowed to bring the peculiar contribution of their nature and experience to the understanding of the Faith and to the living of the Christian life. We have to recover the recognition, lost since Jesus walked on earth, that women in themselves are equally with men part of the Church and that only when men and women are equally persons in the Church will there be any real Christian social life. We have not begun even to recognise how great a task that is and how revolutionary its achievement would be on all our forms of Christian living. For such openings as have been granted to women have but revealed how man-dominated the Church is. Their place is seen as assisting in work already devised and directed by men and not as bringing their own understanding and experience to an enriched development of the Church's life and work. It is only in groups which start from that assumption that any progress can be made. And without such experimenting groups there can be no new life for the Church in this new age.

CONCERN FOR ALL THE ACTIVITIES OF ITS MEMBERS

The second essential which clearly any such group must recognise is concern with the whole of the life of their members in the full scope of their work, of their interests and of their social relationships. This, indeed, follows from the first. If we are concerned with persons we are concerned with all their activities and interests. It is more than a question of our personal relationships with those with whom we live and work. It is the question of our attitude to the activities that they and we are engaged in. Without this interest in the activities themselves personal relationships will remain on the level of individualistic good manners. Conventional good manners depend largely on people keeping their distance from each other. When men are fully committed to each other in a common task good manners have to be transmuted into Christian grace. But it is concern with the purpose of the work that alone has the power to do this.

And the two topics that the Church has regularly eschewed are politics and work. The Church has until recently shown very little interest in the manner of men's work or in its purpose. The leaders of the Churches have indeed in recent years made pronouncements on the Christian 'line' on these subjects. But it is very doubtful whether these pronouncements have in any way affected the life of a congregation. There has been some discussion in congregational groups. There is an uneasy feeling that the teaching of the Church ought to be relevant to these questions. But few men are convinced that the Church is really interested in their jobs for their own sake. The pattern of congregational life has hardly been altered. And yet the part of a man's life which he spends in his work is greater than what he spends on anything else. If it is insignificant in the eyes of the Church, then he is insignificant. The declension from the Reformation doctrine of vocation could not be more complete. The declension from the Church's active concern with the political life of men is just as marked. The area, above all others, in which a man's faith must be seen in action is that of his relationships with those who share his life in town or village. It is there, and there pre-eminently, that he can make his witness; in the ordinary contacts and responsibilities of his local community, in the wider contacts and responsibilities of his nation's life and through that in the world's life. And yet the Church has helped men very little there in an understanding of their situation and in the discharge of their duties. These two subjects—of work and politics—have either been studiously avoided or have been grudgingly touched upon in general platitudes which gain force only when they are misinterpreted from the point of view of the interest of a man's particular class. They have not been enlivened and enlightened by the ardour of faith.

And these two questions touch each other very closely. The problem of work and vocation is a political problem. It raises the whole question of the purpose of our social life. It is the failure to see how our individual work fits in to any purpose which we approve that brings frustration to many men in their work and creates a lack of unity in the community. It is a sense of this purpose and this unity that men are seeking when they ask for an alternative to Communism. They are not looking for a theory or a theology. And our theology is dead unless it gives significance to all the present actions of Christians in all that they are called upon to do. It is useless to ask men to work to the glory of God unless that glory is somehow to be seen in the purpose and the manner of their work. It is not a matter merely of ultimate objectives. It is a matter of social interdependence and of the sense of our personal share of responsibility and enjoyment in the life of the community. Techniques of management and organisation will not solve the problem. There must be a radically new and living conception of the structure of our society and a recognisable articulation of it in the ordinary lives of men. The Christian group cannot be merely a collection of individuals taking their grudging part in the life around them without question and without any unique contribution and finding its specific bond in the things that divide them from their neighbours. It must have a clear sense of its purpose expressed in the ordinary work of its members and in their part in social relationships. That purpose may be expressed mainly in co-operation with the life around them, or it may be expressed in opposition, but that sense of purpose must be there if the group is to survive to any Christian purpose. And so long as the way of co-operation is open—that is, so long as we live in a democracy—the Christian group is called upon to be purposefully concerned with what its members are doing and trying to do in their daily work and with what they are doing and trying to do in that business of living together with other people which we call politics. We, in this country, are at a stage of development when we are, all of us, Christians and others alike, forced to find a new and living manner of social life if the welfare state is not to become an institution trying to meet the selfish desires of individuals. In this business of learning to live as an inter-dependent community, the Church has surely something to say. But its word will have no weight until Christians have begun to find their own answers among themselves and, in their own groups, have shown to men that problems of work and property need not divide but can unite.

FREEDOM OF CHOICE

And this leads directly to the third point. The real weakness of our Christian society is that we have abandoned our freedom of choice. We have allowed others to decide our actions and direct our thoughts for us. We have not come to our opinions and decided our actions because we have humbly and in accordance with our understanding of Christ's demands faced the choices open to us. We have been content to choose between alternatives offered to us by others and have made our choice on their arguments. We make the excuse that we do not know the facts. But the evil is much deeper. For we have given up our freedom of choice in the things that are open and obvious to us. We have allowed others to decide our more personal choices.

Freedom of choice is a burden which some generations have escaped without undue damage to their conscience. But ours is not such an age. A hundred years ago Christians in this country were not greatly troubled in conscience about political problems at home. Perhaps we are amazed that they were not more troubled in their Christian conscience by the slums that they built in the towns and by the conditions in which men were condemned to live and work. They were untroubled because they believed that the area of Christian obedience was a limited area, confined to the domestic life of men. The laws of economics, they thought, left them no freedom of choice. They could be moved to pity and philanthropy but felt themselves faced with no choice in political action. And, of course, they were sustained by hope: by the great hope that economic conditions were bound to get better and better. The standards of Christian ethics were so fully acknowledged and the area of their operation so clearly limited that men could carry on without much question, doing things because they were the things to do. That is the sign of a stable and, perhaps, even of a healthy society: when men do not question the prevailing standards and hypocrisy is easy. It is an entirely different thing to live in an age when consciences are uneasy and when there is no general acceptance of Christian standards. It is, then, a very dangerous thing for Christians to do things merely because other people are doing them. Can we honestly say that there is any obvious difference in the approach of Christians to the ordinary problems of daily living or to the political questions of to-day and the approach of those who could not call themselves Christian ? If we listen to a political discussion between Church members is it in any significant sense different from a similar discussion in a factory or ' pub ' among those who make no profession of the Christian faith ? Are we not as likely to find an approach to a Christian discrimination there as in a Church hall ? Can we not say that the sense of Christian values is as strong outside the Church as within ? For the real problem is not that in this country there is a pagan thinking and a Christian thinking, but that the thinking of all of us is bewildered and what is Christian is not avowedly so. There is nothing for which we should give more hearty thanks to God than that the power of Jesus's teaching has still so great a hold over the minds of ordinary men in this country. There is nothing that should make us in the Church so penitent as the surrender of the Church to ways of thinking of which even the world is ashamed. And the greatest danger there is not to the country but to the Church. Christians must regain their freedom of choice.

It is not a question of all Christians coming to the same decisions and having the same political opinions. Nor is it a question of Christians always opposing or disagreeing with the opinions and actions of others. It is simply the question of Christians choosing their opinions and actions for themselves on their own Christian judgment. There is something very unhealthy in the fact that members of a suburban congregation almost inevitably reflect the political opinion of their neighbourhood and members of an ' industrial ' congregation reflect those of their neighbourhood in so far as they belong to it. The acceptance of our political opinions from those around us is obvious. Our acceptance of their standards in the constant matters of our daily lives is less obvious but more fundamental. For we not only allow others to determine how we shall vote, we allow them to determine how we shall dress, how we shall live and how we shall behave. There was a time when Christians set the standards of their neighbourhood. But the position is now largely reversed. We choose our political opinions as we choose our dress because our neighbours have already chosen. We have to learn to exercise our freedom of choice again. We have to give up the idea that we have done our political duty when we have chosen between the candidates selected for us by others and advocating the policies of parties which contain fewer and fewer Christians. That is not responsible action. We have to get into the parties, to understand the political problems of the day, and, as we learn to understand, to make our contribution in Christian judgment in the working out of policies and in the choice of candidates. But that is not the starting point. If we do not begin to use our freedom of choice in the more mundane matters of daily life we will never rise to making political decisions. For the question of choice is of crucial importance not only to our political life but to our faith. Only as we learn that we can choose will we begin fully to understand our faith and to rejoice in it. It will not be easy. But we do not have to wait. We do not begin by making choices on a world-scale. We do not begin by choosing between peace and war. We have to begin with the choices that are always open to us, with the choices we make every day, often without knowing it. And it's no use if we do that merely as individuals. We have to do it corporately. There must be groups of Christians with the will and the time to consider together how they should choose and to support each other in their decisions. For it is only the group of those who know that they are making their own decisions together and in faith that can withstand persecution—and the most subtle and strongest form of persecution is the domination of ideas. And there is no virtue in being persecuted. Submission to such persecution can come very near to apostasy. When we give up our freedom of choice we have submitted.

When we have given up our freedom of choice we have settled down to live according to the standards of the society around us. We become content if we can serve the purposes of that society and are roused only when the freedom of the Church as an institution is imperilled. We begin by trying to consecrate the way of life in the society around us and end by accepting its standards without much question. And so we forget the difference and the glory of the new life that came to men in Christ. We have to recover the conviction that the Christian Faith is a life to be lived, a social life which has quite distinctive notes. The early Church knew it was the new Community in Christ; its members had all things in common. Benedict, Columba and those who followed the monastic way to Francis and later, knew that one of the things they must give up was the hold that private property had upon them. The Reformers knew that they must make the faith evident in the daily lives of Christians. We may, if we wish, say that their methods were inadequate. But what inspired them was not the adequacy of their schemes but the conviction that the Church was the body of Christ, following His way of life. For them, as for us, the freedom they knew they had to exercise in the use of their material things, not for their own use but for the glory of God.

6. ECONOMIC DISCIPLINE

OUR USE OF MONEY

THE place where we are free to choose and the place where our freedom of decision is most effective is in the use of our money. Many of us are not free to choose how we use our time. The use of most of it is determined by the work we do and few of us are our own masters there. The use of the rest of our time—our leisure time, so called—depends ultimately on the use we make of our money. For the most determining thing in our lives is not our opinions but the way we use our money. It's the way we spend our money that determines the kind of life we live and not, or at least not in the case of most of us, the choice of a particular kind of life that determines how we spend our money. We may think at the start of our adult life that we decide the pattern on which we are going to live but very soon we find that it is determined for us by the things we think we need. That was, presumably, what Jesus meant when He said: " Where your treasure is, there will your heart be also."

THE ABDICATION OF OUR FREEDOM

We may say that we have little choice in the use of our money: that all that we can do is to meet the necessary demands of life for ourselves and our families: that it is only in the use of a diminishing fraction of our money that we have any choice at all. And that, of course, is in a sense true. But it only makes the problem more urgent It shows how unquestioningly we have accepted a standard of life imposed by society as our unalterable pattern of life. It is the clearest demonstration of our unjudging submission to the choices of other people. No suggestion is here made of a lower standard of living. It is rather that our isolated way of living, our fear of any kind of co-operation, our acceptance of customs not because we enjoy them but because they are 'the thing to do,' all make demands on us which become a burden and which other ages have done without. When our financial resources are strained it is all the more necessary that we should choose what we do with them.

And in nothing have we more completely succumbed to the tyranny of individualism than in the avoidance among Christians of any discussion of this. We have inherited from an age of economic individualism the tradition of the stewardship of money. And there are in the Church many who are generous and many who are most disciplined in the personal use of their money. But we have accepted also the tradition that a man's money matters are the one thing that he must not discuss with others. We are willing to discuss our personal prayer life. We are now willing even to discuss our personal relationships. In these ways we have to a certain extent broken down that wall of privacy which prevents any true Christian community. But we have kept the privacy of the purse impregnable. Until we begin to realise that this, the most determining factor in our lives, is something that we must discuss with our fellow-Christians, we cannot hope for any creative social life in the Church. We have to reinterpret the old idea of the stewardship of some of our money in terms of the use of all our money. It is not enough that we should give a proportion of our income 'for the Church,' 'for others,' 'for the Lord.' It is necessary that we see the spending of all our money, especially of that large percentage that is spent on ourselves, as serving or hindering God's purpose. Stewardship, whatever its original meaning—and it is doubtful if it is based on any New Testament teaching except that what a steward uses is never his own and must be accounted for in total—has come to have meaning only for those who have economic security, and to have to do only with the use of one's surplus and to imply that what one spent on oneself and one's family is one's own affair. If our lives are in any sense at all to be lived in the Lord's service, then the question of how we spend our money on our homes, on our children, and on ourselves is really of greater importance than how we spend the residue on others. We shall not begin realistically to discuss together the purpose of our lives and the witness we must make at home and at work until we see the question of the use of all our money as a primary necessity for corporate study and decision. Let us by all means see that we are not allowed to forget our responsibility for others. But that responsibility must be expressed within a fellowship of those who are corporately concerned with what they are doing with the totality of their ordinary lives. It is only thus that our giving for others can be saved from patronage and that love of power which is hidden under a demand for gratitude. And if we are trying to see that the Faith be made intelligible not only to the middle classes but to the working classes, we have to begin to think not in terms of stewardship and charity, for these terms mean nothing, or less than nothing, to the latter with their economic background, but in terms of the use of all our money and of social solidarity. And unless some way is found of bringing Christians together on that level we shall never begin to create a Christian community. We have to learn that our choices are never purely individual choices. We shall learn to choose responsibly what we shall do as persons only as we have learned to understand the purpose of our lives and to find the joy of our lives with other people.

WHERE A CHRISTIAN GROUP MUST BEGIN

There are, then, these three lines which any group which is trying to find the pattern of Christian life to-day must follow. It must be concerned with all the personal relationships of its members. It must be concerned with all the aspects of their lives, especially to-day with their industrial and political lives. And it must be concerned to recover their freedom of choice, especially in the matter of the way they spend their money. These all hang together. But the crux is the last. For that is the determining factor. It is also where we can and must begin.

It is, of course, to open the floodgates to all sorts of problems. We shall find ourselves confronted with all sorts of severely practical questions. We shall have to deal with the question of what we should be doing in the most material problems of our lives and of how we do it. We shall have to face and examine the determined cogency of all the excuses we shall bring forward to justify our continuing in our accustomed ways. We shall find that we shall have to question all that we have taken for granted and it will be very unpleasant. But these are the real questions of our lives. We shall find ourselves confronted also by fundamental questions of justice and equality which such practical discussion will inevitably raise. But these are precisely the demands of the Faith which we consistently evade. We shall, indeed, be forced at last to ask what loving one another means. And only a group which somehow has had a glimpse of the love of Christ and has a real desire to pursue it will be able to hold together. But we must be prepared to find that many unexpected people know that love though they would not care to describe it in theological terms.

The first necessity of such a group, which will find itself with plenty to discuss, is to take the first step from discussion to action. There must be some quite practical and material means by which their concern for these issues is, from the first, expressed in action. As the crux is in our use of our money and as the main obstacle is the deeply entrenched doctrine of the privacy of the purse, that first action must take the form of some definite scheme of joint responsibility for cash contributed by all members of the group and used corporately by the group and in the name of the group. There will be no reality until each member hands over some money and the group handles it corporately. It is better to begin with that, even in a token way, than to keep discussion going till we find a bigger and a better scheme, which answers all our questions and solves all our problems. Discussion is often a drug that we indulge in as the best preventitive of all action. The first step in positive action, however trivial it seems, is more creative than the understanding that comes from the fullest discussion. Unless we find the way to take that first step we remain in the realm of theory.

EXPERIMENTS THAT HAVE BEEN MADE: THE SHADWELL GROUP

There are many groups who have taken and are taking a first step in various ways. The Shadwell Group in particular has been a pioneer both in actual experiment and in explanation of the need of it. They adopted as the standard income for all members of the group the national average income, with allowances for a wife and children. They felt that the national average income was the income that a man was entitled to use for himself and for his own purposes. Any expenditure above that had to be explained and justified to the group. Those who received more in actual income than the national average put the balance into a common fund used by the decision of the group itself, first, for the relief of any members whose income was under the national average and, secondly, for the support of any work or cause that the group approved. This forthright experiment raised for the group all sorts of practical problems. Its strength lay in the fact that it took account of the economic position of the rest of the nation and that the group itself had made an act of judgment in deciding on the national average as the standard for their lives. They made their own choice in terms of justice and equality.

Critics might claim that the national average is a purely fictitious figure: that our neighbours do not live on the national average but on a range of income above and below, and that by living on the national average level oneself one can have very little effect on others. But the real importance of the Shadwell Group's experiment was in their free choice of a standard of life for themselves and in the inter-dependence and joint responsibility that this scheme forced on them.*

THE SCHEME OF THE IONA COMMUNITY

The Iona Community owes a great deal to the example and inspiration of the Shadwell Group. But the scheme of economic discipline on which they are now embarked is much slighter. The Shadwell Group came into existence for the precise purpose of making this economic experiment. The Iona Community has found the need of an economic discipline as it has faced the task of the Church in the world to-day and the demands of its own community life. The scheme with which it now experiments seems a more practicable first step for a larger group which is already in existence. The Community was also anxious to find a way of economic discipline which could be used not only in their more close-knit body but in groups of more varied composition—of Minister and Women Associates and of young people—with a wide variety of economic positions. By this scheme,† each member contributes to a common fund a percentage of his 'disposable income.' 'Disposable income' is a man's income after deductions have been made for Income Tax, Rent and allowances. For the sake of simplicity the allowances are taken as the Income Tax allowances given by the Inland Revenue for a wife and children, for working expenses, etc.: with the exception of the personal allowance which is the same

* *The National Average* by Lex Miller.
† For details see Appendix I.

for everyone. The money thus contributed is used by the decision of the group itself for the relief of members in difficulty and for purposes chosen by the group. This scheme takes no serious account of the wide divergence in income within the group. Those who have most contribute most but are also left with most. Thus it takes no serious account of justice and equality. But the scheme is adopted because it is a practical first step. It is a minimum step and practical for any group which has a serious desire to begin some kind of corporate economic witness. And its strength is in the necessity of corporate sharing of one's economic problems and in corporate responsibility for the spending of money. It expresses that economic interdependence on which any Christian social life must be built, even if it expresses it only in a token way. If the group is serious it will soon find that it is involved in greater issues and must go forward or disband.

In each critical stage of the world's history men in the Church have had to face one question. That question did not always take the same form, though basically it was the question as to whether they took Christ seriously. The question was a vital and practical question for each man who heard it. In the early days of the Church it was the simple question as to whether he would give up the old life to which he was accustomed and enter the strange and new family of the faith. And the question still comes in that form to men to-day in Asia and Africa. In the beginning of the Dark Ages men and women had to decide whether for love of Christ and in obedience to His Way they would give up their ordinary life and enter the social life of a monastery. Many did not and no one blames them. But those who did saved Europe. They did not know to what their action would lead and did not care. They knew only that they must decide this personal question in this way. In the age of the Reformation men had to decide whether they would make the faith a living thing in their homes and daily lives. Only a few perhaps knew what they were doing. But they changed the life of our country.

How does the question come to us to-day? It does not matter that everyone does not hear it in the same way. The only thing that matters for us is whether we refuse or obey. We do not know what the world will be like. We do not know what the future form of the Church will be. And we need not worry. But we can be sure that God is putting one question to us. We cannot excape that question for it is forced on us by what is happening in the world, in our country and in our homes. We know that our obedience involves our seeking a fuller life with others, with our fellow-Christians and with other men, and that it depends in the first instance on our free personal choice.

But not on that choice alone, as if everything depends on us. The choice will lead to new tasks and to the joy of discovering the fullness of the faith in our life together. For it is God Who works and He works through men. The men who chose the monastic life found themselves involved in the work of creating a new society. The men of the Reformation found themselves involved in creating a new Scotland. They knew in their own lives that Christ was King. There were only a few of them at first. There will perhaps only be a few groups now. But it has to begin.

7. THE HEART OF THE MATTER

THE last word must be quite practical. We have been thinking in terms of a new pattern of life in a world Church. Such thinking sounds grandiose. We must remember that at the beginning it will mean simply small groups of people discussing together their own problems and coming to decisions about their own lives.

Such groups will be dealing with very mundane matters and their members will feel perhaps rather the burden of the trivial than the uplift of a great adventure. We have got to be prepared for the questions which we ourselves shall bring up.

All through this essay we've used the word 'pattern.' We have become so isolated in our Christian obedence that almost inevitably the pattern which we seek will again and again be in danger of being thought of as the pattern for individuals and therefore a uniform pattern for each of us. But we shall only fully know the joy and peace of Christian obedience when we see the pattern as one into which our individual lives are fitted.

For we are not trying to build community. We can never do that. God sets us in community and it is man's sin that he is always breaking it. God has set us in inescapable community, in our family, in our neighbourhood, in all the relationships with others that life brings. And all the time we rebel. All the time we kick against the pricks. When we are enlivened by the Spirit of Christ we accept community and begin to live according to the laws of our being.

The New Testament and especially the Epistles are full of pictures which are there expressly to help men to know that new life in Christ in such a pattern of the whole and not of the atoms. For many of us who go to Iona one of these metaphors has been vividly exemplified in the walls of the Abbey itself. As we sit at worship the boulder-built walls—the mediaeval masonry—of the Abbey faces us. The pink and darker red granite blocks of all sizes, little round stones and parallel blue slabs of slates, of which the walls are built, give to us a picture of the variety and dissimilarity of the 'lively stones' of the Temple of which we seek to be a part.

With such a picture of the pattern we seek clearly in our minds, we shall be recalled from two dangers: the pursuit of uniformity and the complacence of legalism. The 'lively stones' are not to be concrete slabs and as we seek to form our lives to the gifts and needs of others joined with us in the service of Christ we are not likely to feel that we have attained.

For what is going to happen when such a group as we have been describing gets together to discuss how its members spend their money and how they can manage to contribute to a common fund? The questions will be quite inevitable: 'How can I give more than I am already committed to giving?' 'I don't see how I can do what so-and-so is giving:' 'I cannot join this group because I am not so disciplined as the others, or because I am so much more, or so much less than they.' Behind all these questions and doubts will be the assumption that there is a basic pattern into which we have all to fit. Either we'll assume that what we see as the pattern, or even what we're doing, is *the* pattern for everyone else, or, more probably, we'll see some other's pattern as *the* pattern and know that we can never fit into it, or, worst of all, we'll try to. And the real crux of our difficulties will be about our families. If we were solitary individuals we might force ourselves into a new *mould*. But we are members of families. Our economic life is bound up with that of the other members of our families and is governed by all kinds of individual and corporate needs and tasks. We cannot draw ourselves out of our families and we know we can't force them into an artificial pattern. And we don't want to do either.

These will be the kind of questions we shall ask because even though we dislike this idea of uniformity, we can hardly think in any other terms.

Equality has a profound meaning for Christians but it does not mean that. When Peter had heard from Jesus what life still held for him, he asked what was to happen to John. Jesus answered: " What is that to thee ? " And that answer and rebuke has an eternal meaning for us.

In our groups we must have a full and deepening recognition of the varieties of personality and calling with their varying needs and characteristics. There is nothing in the Gospels to suggest that Jesus had a uniform standard which he applied to all men. What disconcerted men was the wide variety of the ways in which He treated men. They could not reduce His treatment of men to a recognisable pattern. He treated each differently, because He treated all fully as persons. That was what was common in His treatment of all. That was His pattern and it bewildered men.

We shall go wrong if because of our need to find a new way of social living we try to impose a rigid pattern on others. It is the thing we all tend to do and it is the death of community. At this stage of history it is urgent that we learn imaginatively to see Christian community. For we have gained for the individual a new freedom which is almost terrifying. Men find themselves individually free in a way unknown to previous generations. It is this sense of freedom that makes men to-day lost and often lonely. It is this that makes many turn to any authority that takes their freedom from them. It will be tragic if the Church now seeks to impose a new individual pattern. It is easy to regret the slackening of codes because it is so much easier to have them. It is easy to regret the slackening of the authority of the family. It is misleading to stress too much the rising rate of divorce and take no account of unhappy Victorian families and sons—so many—often the best sons—driven from home. We have to remember the price paid for the rigidity of the pattern that is broken. And we have to be very careful not to try to impose another pattern of a different mould but of equal rigidity.

For the adventure to which we are called does not mean giving up, but entering into our own.

We are relying on Jesus' promise that the one gift no man can take from us, the one gift that must be full, is joy, and His joy can be known only as we are together with other men in Him. It is that joy of a larger, purposeful fellowship which will help our children to enter into the wider life of men, which is no slackening of family ties but rather the means by which they grow and become mature. And it is this natural and joyful sharing of a common life which alone will be a winning pattern for other men.

APPENDIX I

THE IONA COMMUNITY'S SCHEME OF ECONOMIC DISCIPLINE

THE basis of the scheme is that each member contributes a percentage of his disposable income to a common fund which is used for purposes chosen by the corporate decision of the Community.

The scheme is based on the Income Tax return of each member. Practically everyone has to make such a return. The allowances granted are on the same scale for all. One's disposable income is found by deducting from one's total income Income Tax paid, Rent and Rates (or, in the case of someone owning the house in which he lives, assessed rental and rates) and all Income Tax allowances except the personal allowance. The personal allowance is excepted because it is the same for all and our discipline must be concerned with what we spend on ourselves. A percentage of this disposable income is paid in a common fund which, by the decision of the group, is used to help members in financial difficulty and to support what work or causes they desire.

In the Community itself, the percentage paid is 5%. This assumes that members are giving another 5% for their Church and other Christian liberality and that therefore they are using at least 10% of their disposable income for others.

Some rulings have been made :—

1. Those who for some particular reason cannot undertake the 5% are allowed to make a contribution according to their means.
2. When a member is committed to giving in other Christian liberality more than 5% of his disposable

income he may deduct that extra from his contribution to the Community fund.
3. Where a Minister lives alone and has to keep a housekeeper, he is allowed an extra allowance. This is the only allowance not given by the Inland Revenue which is allowed.
4. When the wife of a member wishes to join a similar group (Women Associates) the 5% of their disposable joint income would be divided between them.

The Minister Associates and the Women Associates of the Community have adopted a similar rule but have made the percentage $2\frac{1}{2}$%. As this is a new idea for the Associates, it has not been made an obligatory part of their rule. But a good proportion of them have formed groups to make the experiment on behalf of the Association. "The Committed Family"—a group of young people in Community House, Glasgow—have adopted the $2\frac{1}{2}$%. The members of The Christian Workers' League pay 5% of their incomes into a common fund to maintain their work.

Examples*

1. A minister with a wife and two children: a stipend of £800 and a manse and no private income.

    The allowances allowed him for Income Tax are:—
    - (a) For his wife £120
    - (b) For his two children 200
    - (c) For National Insurance 18
    - (d) For expenses 40
    - (e) For his own Insurances (including Widow's Fund) 20

       Total of Allowances £398

* As at October, 1958.

APPENDIX I

He pays no rent but he pays £10 in Income Tax. Add this £10 to his allowances. The total is now £408.

Deduct this from his income: £800 — £408. The balance, which we call his disposable income, is £392. 5% of this is £20.

2. A married man with two children—

Income	£600	0	0
Allowances:—			
National Insurance ... £18 0 0			
Allowance for Wife ... 120 0 0			
Allowance for Children 200 0 0			
Rent 50 0 0			
Tax Paid 4 0 0			
Total to be deducted ...	392	0	0
Residue after deduction	£208	0	0
Upon this residue 5 % should be calculated			
5% of £208	£10	0	0

3. A single woman living at home—Income £380 0 0

Allowance:—			
National Insurance ... £18 0 0			
Approximation of Rent ... 26 0 0			
Tax Paid 42 0 0			
Total to be deducted	86	0	0
Residue after deduction	£294	0	0
5% of £294	£14	14	0

APPENDIX II

BIBLIOGRAPHY

THIS bibliography mentions only those books which were found relevant to the subject of this book. Inevitably the background literature is too vast for any one person to tackle and his general reading too scrappy and unremembered to be recorded.

It cannot be said that there is any authoritative work dealing in any definite way with the subject of the changing pattern of the Church's life: at least I have found none. Of books that have helped in that general survey particular mention must be made of K. S. Latourette's *History of the Expansion of Christianity* (6 vols.) and E. Troeltsch's *The Social Teaching of the Christian Churches* (2 vols.). Other books that have helped are, Lewis Mumford's *Condition of Man*, A. G. Hebert's *The Form of the Church*, John MacMurray's *The Clue to History*, Alan Richardson's *Christian Apologetics*, F. J. Leenhardt's *Christianisme et Vie Publique*, Sir Alexander Gray's *The Socialist Tradition: from Moses to Lenin*, G. M. Trevelyan's *Social History of England* and Lex Miller's *Biblical Politics*.

It is surprising how little is written about the life of the early Church when we consider how much has been written about its thinking. A. Harnack's *The Expansion of Christianity in the First Three Centuries* is still a source of much information. R. Newton Flew's *Jesus and His Church* and T. R. Glover's *The Ancient World* were helpful.

Of the Dark Ages and the rise of monasticism, in addition to primary sources such as *The Rule of St. Benedict*, particular mention should be made of Christopher Dawson's *Christianity and the Rise of Western Culture*, Sir Maurice Powicke's *Christian Life in the Middle Ages*, Dom Columba

Elwes' *Law, Liberty and Love*, G. G. Coulton's *Scottish Abbeys and Social Life*.

Of the Middle Ages: Dom David Knowles' *The Religious Orders in England*, Moorman's *Church Life in England in the Thirteenth Century*, G. R. Owst's *Preaching in Mediaeval England*, A. G. Hebert's *Liturgy and Society*, R. F. Bennet's *The Early Dominicans*.

Of the Reformation: R. H. Tawney's *Religion and the Rise of Capitalism*, H. M. Robertson's *Aspects of the Rise of Economic Individualism*, Alfred von Matrin's *Sociology of the Renaissance*, E. Rosenstock Huesy's *The Christian Future*, A. D. Lindsay's *The Modern Democratic State*, and *The Essentials of Democracy*, A. S. R. Woodhouses' *Puritanism and Liberty* and W. R. Forrester's *Protestant Ethics and the Spirit of Capitalism* (in Expository Times).

Of the Industrial Revolution and after: E. Halevy's *History of the English People*, J. L. and Barbara Hammond's *The Bleak Age* and *The Age of the Chartists*, K. Polanyi's *Origin of our Time*, A. Vidler's *The Orb and the Cross*, A. D. Lindsay's *Christianity and Economics*—and, of course, the biographies and novels of the time.

For Scotland: Tom Johnston's *The History of the Working Classes in Scotland* is invaluable: also L. J. Saunder's *Scottish Democracy*: 1815-1840 and C. A. Oakley's *Second City*. The Memoirs of Norman Macleod and other biographies give a picture of the life of the Church in Scotland.

Books on the contemporary situation are legion. Special mention should be made of G. F. MacLeod's *We Shall Rebuild* and, of more recent books, of Leslie Hunter's *Church Strategy in a Changing World* and John MacMurray's *Conditions of Freedom*.

On Church life on the mission field: *The Economic Basis of the Church*: Tambaram Report, Vol. 5, and J. Merle Davis' *The Economic and Social Environment of the Younger Churches* and articles in the *International Review of Missions*.

Of contemporary experiments: see the publications of the Oecumenical Institute, particularly *Professional Life as Christian Vocation* (No III) and *Contribution to a Social Ethic* (No. IV): the publications of the " Centre Protestant d'Etudes " at Geneva and of the Study Department of the World Council of Churches. For the Shadwell Group's Experiment, Lex Miller's *The National Average: a Study in Social Discipline*.

THE IONA COMMUNITY IS:

- An ecumenical movement of men and women from different walks of life and different traditions in the Christian church
- Committed to the gospel of Jesus Christ, and to following where that leads, even into the unknown
- Engaged together, and with people of goodwill across the world, in acting, reflecting and praying for justice, peace and the integrity of creation
- Convinced that the inclusive community we seek must be embodied in the community we practise

Together with our staff, we are responsible for:
- Our islands residential centres of Iona Abbey, the MacLeod Centre on Iona, and Camas Adventure Centre on the Ross of Mull

and in Glasgow:
- The administration of the Community
- Our work with young people
- Our publishing house, Wild Goose Publications
- Our association in the revitalising of worship with the Wild Goose Resource Group

The Iona Community was founded in Glasgow in 1938 by George MacLeod, minister, visionary and prophetic witness for peace, in the context of the poverty and despair of the Depression. Its original task of rebuilding the monastic ruins of Iona Abbey became a sign of hopeful rebuilding of community in Scotland and beyond. Today, we are about 250 Members, mostly in Britain, and 1500 Associate Members, with 1400 Friends worldwide. Together and apart, 'we follow the light we have, and pray for more light'.

For information on the Iona Community contact:
The Iona Community, Fourth Floor, Savoy House, 140 Sauchiehall Street,
Glasgow G2 3DH, UK. Phone: 0141 332 6343
e-mail: ionacomm@gla.iona.org.uk; web: www.iona.org.uk

For enquiries about visiting Iona, please contact:
Iona Abbey, Isle of Iona, Argyll PA76 6SN, UK. Phone: 01681 700404
e-mail: ionacomm@iona.org.uk

Wild Goose Publications, the publishing house of the Iona Community established in the Celtic Christian tradition of Saint Columba, produces books, tapes and CDs on:

- holistic spirituality
- social justice
- political and peace issues
- healing
- innovative approaches to worship
- song in worship, including the work of the Wild Goose Resource Group
- material for meditation and reflection

If you would like to find out more about our books, tapes and CDs, please contact us at:

Wild Goose Publications
Fourth Floor, Savoy House
140 Sauchiehall Street,
Glasgow G2 3DH, UK

Tel. +44 (0)141 332 6292
Fax +44 (0)141 332 1090
e-mail: admin@ionabooks.com

or visit our website at
www.ionabooks.com
for details of all our products and online sales